THE WOMAN MVP WHO SET YOU FREE

CHAPTER ONE
Making the Cut

CHAPTER TWO
In the Big Leagues

CHAPTER THREE
You Don't Major in the Minors

CHAPTER FOUR
Season Training

CHAPTER FIVE
Following the Rule Book

CHAPTER SIX
The Playing Field

CHAPTER SEVEN
Running the Ball

CHAPTER EIGHT
The Refs Call It

CHAPTER NINE
The Playoffs

CHAPTER TEN
Who Moved the Goal Posts?

CHAPTER ELEVEN
Winning the Game

CHAPTER TWELVE
You Did It!

Meet Business and Life Coach
LuAn Halter F.A.B.I.
The Woman MVP who set you Free
Play Quarterback with the big boys and WIN!
LuAn Halter, F.A.B.I.

LuAn Mitchell-Halter knows business. With long experience as one of the most accomplished women in the world, she has an intimate understanding of the issues of competitiveness and global pressures on the "playing field" in today's tough "business of life" world. In fact, McGill University presented her with their Management Achievement Award in 2003 and she was named Canada's Number One Female Entrepreneur by Profit and Chatelaine magazines in a nationwide search, for THREE consecutive years!

As a strong believer of building a better planet one person at a time, she takes her "seeds for good" and endeavors to plant this knowledge and experience across the globe. Here in the woman MVP that set you Free, she relays the messages we all need to achieve our greatest heights.

As a highly sought after motivational speaker, international bestselling author and first-class personality LuAn is known around the planet for her inspiring message of perseverance and triumph.

Through affiliations with the likes of the Leading Women Entrepreneurs of the World—she was inducted in 2001, and hosted the annual gala in 2005—*Chicken Soup for the Soul's* Mark Victor Hansen and the *Most Amazing Charles" Tremendous" Jones, Books are Tremendous !*

LuAn works hard with like-minded individuals to plant "seeds of good" around our beautiful planet. She has helped others reach their true potential, and she can help you!

Every year since 1998, LuAn awards a deserving student with the Fred Mitchell Memorial Scholarship, which provides young, at risk people with an opportunity to create a better life. People between the ages of 17 and 21 years old who have worked with a community partner, agency or program to turn their lives around are eligible for this scholarship.

LuAn is also the first to roll up her shirtsleeves to help global efforts, and has given millions to worthy causes.

She keeps active on many outside boards.

LuAn is a member of the Women's Leadership Board at the JFK School of Government, Harvard University—this international board of more than 100 women work together to increase the visibility, participation and influence of women worldwide.

She also sits on the University of Saskatchewan's Institute of Agricultural, Rural, and Environmental Health, Canada's only organization devoted to health issues in agriculture.

Advancing Canadian Entrepreneurship welcomed LuAn to their board in 2004. ACE is a national, not-for-profit organization that works with businesses and higher education to organize teams of university students to teach the values and principles or entrepreneurship and market economics.

Woman MVP Wisdom teaches you to believe in yourself, and your dreams. Everything you need to achieve your biggest of big dreams, everything you need to succeed, everything you need to be happy—the instinct, the guts and the drive—are already deep inside you, just waiting to burst out and grow into a garden of beautiful blessings.

LuAn shows you how to use those passionate feelings to become a success!

The American Biographical Institute, USA, one of the leading authorities on the biographies of distinguished individuals worldwide, named LuAn its Woman of the Year 2005, and awarded her the "Lifetime Achievement Award" for 2006.

She was also invited to be a Fellow of the ABI.

LuAn currently lives with her husband, Dr. Reese Halter, and their three children in Rancho Mirage, CA, and Banff, Alberta.

In 2004, she released the powerful international bestselling book, *Paper Doll: Lessons Learned from a Life Lived in the Headlines*, and continues her work as a sensational communicator, motivational speaker, and author and seminar leader. Now available also on CD!

LuAn's latest on paperback is the newly released *Lessons learned by the Impossible Dreamer.*

And she is featured with "all time" Greats like Zig Ziglar, Brian Tracy and Jim Rohn in *Self Growth's 101 Ways to Improve your life!*

Les Hewitt's *Power of Focus,* and Gord Carley's *Overcoming Adversity* have featured LuAn one of the World's top experts as a business and Life Coach!

The six-hour *Eye of the Tiger* CD series and workbook, based on surefire strategies for a rewarding life that we all deserve, and LuAn's fantastic new seminar series for business professionals, *Climb Every Mountain,* are just two of the valuable components of her mission and dedication to us all.

For much more ... Please visit LuAn at:
www.eyeofthetiger.us
www.paperdoll.net
www.climbeverymountain.us
www.LuAnMitchell.com
www.thewomanmvp.com

LuAn takes to the field
The Time is NOW!
Come On Girls… Let's "Just do IT!"
and Do it Good!

Let's start with an "awareness," exercise, that we will ponder as we read, and begin creating our very own Woman MVP images from the "inside and out," let's take to the field "beauty tips."
Please give some thought to this wonderful poem by an
Unforgettable woman MVP
Audrey Hepburn
She wrote this poem when asked to share her "beauty tips." It was read at her funeral years later.

For attractive lips, speak words of kindness…
For lovely eyes, seek out the good in people.
For a slim figure, share your food with the hungry.
For beautiful hair, let a child run his/her fingers through it once a day.
For poise, walk with the knowledge that you never walk alone…
People, even more than things, have to be restored, renewed, revived, reclaimed, and redeemed; never throw out anyone.
Remember, if you ever need a helping hand, you will find one at the end of each of your arms.
As you grow older, you will discover that you have two hands; one for helping yourself, and the other for helping others.

NOTE: YOU WILL RETURN HERE AT THE END OF THE BOOK!

Message from LuAn Mitchell-Halter

Now, Let's Begin on "solid ground" to "build" upon, a Winning game plan...let's find some "Coaches!" and get "Changed" for the Game!

Let's, begin by taking a moment out to "get in a Winner's mindset."

M — (My)

Your opponent, in the end, is never really the player on the other side of the net, or the swimmer in the next lane, or the team on the other side of the field, or even the bar you must high-jump. Your opponent is yourself, your negative internal voices, your level of determination.

–Grace Lichtenstein American Writer & Editor

V — (Victory)

Men forget everything; women remember everything. That's why men need instant replays in sports. They've already forgotten what happened.

–Rita Rudner

P — (Plan)

Sports Do Not Build Character...They Reveal It

–John Wooden

If you can't accept losing, you can't win.

–Vince Lombardi

I was never a bookworm. I remember reading Dr. Seuss, the Hardy Boys, Emil and the Detectives, Chip Hilton, and lots of Mark Twain and Dickens. My athletic ability did nothing but invite taunts. I was an indifferent student and an athlete with delusions of adequacy, dreams of adulation.

–John Grisham

Champions aren't made in gyms. Champions are made from something they have deep inside them-a desire, a dream, and a vision. They have to have last-minute stamina, they have to be a little faster, and they have to have the skill and the will. But the will must be stronger than the skill.

–Muhammad Ali

If a woman has to choose between catching a fly ball and saving an infant's life, she will choose to save the infant's life without even considering if there is a man on base.

–Dave Barry

When I step onto the court, I don't have to think about anything. If I have a problem off the court, I find that after I play, my mind is clearer and I can come up with a better solution. It's like therapy. It relaxes me and allows me to solve problems.

–Michael Jordan

Doctors and scientists said that breaking the four-minute mile was impossible, that one would die in the attempt. Thus, when I got up from the track after collapsing at the finish line, I figured I was dead.

–Roger Bannister (After becoming the first person to break the four-minute mile, 1952)

Outline

Always remember Goliath was a 40 point favorite over David.

–Shug Jordan

Introduction

You're the "Athlete" this world's been waiting for. Being a woman has never been better.

Corporate business and The "playing field" of LIFE—much like professional Sports—is a tough game full of cheap shots and winning plays. Being a woman quarterback playing with a rulebook you don't understand and no strategy for playing the field… makes it even tougher to win. Learn the rules of the game and become the Most Valuable Person—MVP—in your life. The key is choosing the right path and the right team to help you win the Super Bowl of life.

In the Woman MVP, LuAn Mitchell-Halter tells how successful businesswomen and athletes won the big game, and shares the triumphant stories of women Mitchell-Halter admires most. Their inspirational stories taught Mitchell-Halter how to attain her own success, and now she passes them onto other women in a voice that is unique only to her. Woman MVP stands out because it serves as a journal and workbook for anyone chasing a dream. Mitchell-Halter encourages readers to adapt her tips and lessons to their own goal through fun exercises and questions that every MVP needs to ask herself.

Mitchell-Halter's signature blend of frank observations and humorous anecdotes lend a playful twist to a serious lesson in winning the game of life.

Each chapter is dedicated to a common obstacle today's woman faces and with it, the story of successful women who tackled barriers and opened the playing field for "Life Long" success. COACH'S CORNER wisdom will carry the day as new Women MVP's take to the field! This book is not a platform for bashing … but instead celebrates women, their challenges and most of all, their achievements.

"Wonder" Women are playing alongside the "Big" boys, not against them. In addition to the outstanding achievements and men highlighted in this book, LuAn will feature some "Wonder Women" and "big boys" that have had great influence in her life! Please watch for the "Wonder Women" and "Big Boys" all throughout the book, and even make a list of your own for future reference!

This is a book for anyone who has ever wanted to win, and everyone who is already a winner. Mitchell Halter enlightens the reader and offers solutions that bring success in a Fun and easy to Understand "Action Plan!" So, Come on, it's time to "Hit the Field!" And please, remember to keep a little humor and "go with the flow," while we are at it!

CHAPTER ONE
MAKING THE CUT

Obstacle to overcome: EGO

M — (My)

Most of the shadows of this life are caused by standing in one's own sunshine.

—Ralph Waldo Emerson

V — (Victory)

The nice thing about egotists is that they don't talk about other people.

—Lucille S. Harper

P — (Plan)

You probably wouldn't worry about what people think of you if you could know how seldom they do.

—Olin Miller

Life and business, both, can be a tough game full of cheap shots and winning plays—but if you learn the rules of the game, you can become the MVP on any playing field, and it can only get better!

John Elway—the NFL quarterback great who led his team to two consecutive Super Bowl wins in 1998 and 1999—told *Sports Illustrated* after his second win, "I never thought it could get any better than last year but look at this scene. I never, ever thought I would be Super Bowl MVP."

It isn't easy for anyone to picture being MVP, but the first step is envisioning your dream and making a game plan to achieve it. You are the quarterback—you are in control of calling the plays and shaping the way your game plays out.

So how do you make the cut?

The key is mental toughness. It's difficult to define mental toughness because it means something different for each person, and the definition is always evolving. Vince Lombardi once summed it up when he said, *"Mental toughness is many things. It is humility because it behooves all of us to remember that simplicity is the sign of greatness and meekness is the sign of true strength. Mental toughness is spartanism with qualities of sacrifice, self-denial, dedication. It is fearlessness, and it is love."*

What does seem to be a common thread in defining mental toughness is the qualities of those who have it.

Motivation - What is your goal and more importantly, how badly do you want to achieve your goal? The more you want something, the harder you will work to get it. Be careful that your motivation isn't misplaced. For example, do not say you are dieting and assuming an extreme exercise regime because you want to be healthier, when in fact you're hoping your new hot body will land you Mr. Right. Be honest with yourself and make sure you have a clear goal. It's a lot easier working toward something that is important to you.

Commitment - Motivation also helps you develop a strong commitment to achieving your goal. It's one thing to be excited over a defined goal, and another to act upon that excitement. What good is it to make a plan for starting your own business if you never actually plan on carrying through with it? Make sure that you are willing to do what it takes to achieve your goal. There are no benchwarmers allowed on this winning team!

Tenacity - Despite all of your preparation and hard work, you are going to encounter adversity in pursuit of your dream. It is how you cope with this adversity that will demonstrate your true mental strength. Do you crack and give up at the first sign of hard times, or are you more motivated to overcome obstacles?

When a football player takes a hard hit in the Super Bowl, he does not call it a day and go home. He/she picks themselves up and finds a way to prevent that from happening again.

Focus - When adversity is slapping you around, it's important to remain focused on your goal and why you want it so much. Losers dwell, winners excel. Do not concentrate on all of the things you've done wrong. Learn from them and use those lessons to move forward keeping your eye on the ball.

When Women wanted to play professional football, they did NOT sign up and start saving for a Sex change so they could "make" the cut, instead they started their own Pro Football league!

Here is an example of "Women in Football":

The Long Beach AfterShock, a women's professional football team, take great pride in being a part of many communities. We are women, football players, female athletes, moms, Californians; the list goes on and on. We also see ourselves as part of the Long Beach Community.

The Damsels are a dance squad comprised of young ladies ages 12-17, who have been selected to perform at halftime for the Long Beach Aftershock. The Damsels represent various cities, including

Los Angeles, Carson and Gardena. These young ladies show great style, charisma and personality. Their enthusiasm and rhythmic dance moves make for an entertaining and fun show.

With motivation, commitment and tenacity and completely on purpose the dance squad is creating an interest in performing arts by using dancing as a tool to expose youths and their families to the physical, mental and educational benefits of performing arts. The generosity and support of the Long Beach Aftershock have allowed many of the youths involved in the Damsels the opportunity to improve their self-esteem and skill level by performing for the first time in their lives in front to of a public audience.

I was thrilled to meet (and get a real BEAR HUG) from one of the professional female quarterbacks who "made the cut" for women's professional football after one of my talks to the eWomen's network!

She made me aware of the existence and "Power Plays" of these athletic dynamos!

This excerpt on WOMEN IN SPORTS, U.S. Society and Values,
   Dated: December 2003
   This report provides much insight for us in her extensive online detail located at: usinfo.state.gov/journals/itsv/1203/ijse/smith.htm
   Written and researched by Claire Smith

Girls and women are participating as never before in all levels of organized sports in the United States, thanks to changing public attitudes and a landmark piece of federal legislation. Event was merely new women's ran.

When C. Vivian Stringer, in the beginning stages of what has become a Hall of Fame career, saw her women's basketball team from tiny Cheyney State College in

Pennsylvania qualify in 1982 for the first-ever women's national championship sanctioned by the National Collegiate Athletic Association (NCAA), it was like reaching for the moon.

If the event was merely new and uncharted territory for the NCAA, the leading organization that governs intercollegiate athletics in the United States and that, for years, had sponsored every high-profile men's championship tournament, it was unprecedented in women's ranks.

Even for the most celebrated names in women's basketball, achievements had always occurred well under the radar of major college men's sports, with their generous donors and revenue-earning television exposure. So to qualify for that first championship, Stringer's team had to, well, get there.

The road from rural south eastern Pennsylvania to the inaugural event, held on the Norfolk, Virginia, campus of Old Dominion University, had many stops along the way for bake sales, raffles, pleas for donations, and any other fundraising technique Stringer and the team from the historically black college could devise.

"I remember going to a church to solicit money so that we could have little white C's sewn on our sweaters so we'd look nice getting on airplanes," Stringer said of the long road to that first title game in which Cheyney State lost to storied Louisiana Tech. "A sporting goods store volunteered to give us uniforms so that we'd have more than one set. Our administration solicited local companies. On campus, there was as much a fear of our being successful than not, because there was always the thought, "How are we going to pay to go to the next round?" "Now, fast-forward to the year 2000. Stringer was coaching her current team, nationally ranked Rutgers University in Piscataway, New Jersey. When Rutgers upset the University of Georgia in the NCAA Western Conference finals, it meant a third trip for Stringer to the "final four"—the championship round of games involving the four surviving teams. By then, the coach learned, the mode of transportation for such teams was very much first-class in every way.

Media and Crowds

Life at the top for such women's teams, at the dawn of the 21st century, was nothing short of top-of-the-line. Women athletes not only had access to national television audiences—and national television funding—but also expected, and received, staples that once were the sole province of the men's basketball teams. These included, in addition to major media coverage, custom-built team buses, chartered air travel, first-rate hotel lodging and—not the least of the benefits—loyal fan bases. In fact, the "final four" destination in 2000 was not a sleepy college campus, but metropolitan Philadelphia, Pennsylvania, where a sparkling new professional sports facility, with its 20,000 seats, stood ready to receive the women athletes and their enthusiastic followers. Capacity crowds turned out to see not only Rutgers, but also several superlative, nationally renowned squads—such as the University of Tennessee and the University of Connecticut, the modern-day basketball dynasty that has become something akin to the Beatles of a generation ago when it comes to popularity among prepubescent girls. Nationally televised in prime time, the two-day weekend event was completely sold out. The semi-final round brought out the largest crowd ever to ever see a college game—women's or men's—in Pennsylvania's history, as well as a record number of reporters, sportscasters, and other members of the media. Looking back, Stringer, now a member of the Women's Basketball Hall of Fame recalls that weekend as a major development. "To walk in and see that giant arena filled, to see the impact of the sport in Philadelphia and elsewhere, was something you never would have dreamed of in 1982," she said. Women's sports have changed dramatically on so many levels in recent decades. To be sure, there have been bumps in the road; one was the recent demise of the professional Women's United Soccer Association the result of low revenue and sagging ticket sales. Yet despite such setbacks, the growth of women's sports—from youth programs to secondary school and university levels and on to professional leagues and competitions—can only be described as phenomenal. Surely, tennis legends Althea Gibson and Billie Jean King never might have envisioned the success, worldwide recognition, and unprecedented earnings of today's women tennis stars like Serena and Venus Williams. Legendary golfer Babe Didrikson Zaharias could not have foreseen the explosion in popularity of women's golf, with its galaxy of international stars such as Annika Sorenstam of Sweden and Se Ri Pak of South Korea.

COACH'S CORNER
Give some ongoing thought to this article as you read on throughout the entire—Woman MVP—book

'Women's Professional Basketball'

A stunning example is the professional Women's National Basketball Association (WNBA). It exists with glitter and glamour that girls could not have imagined 30 years ago, in major-league cities and state-of-the-art arenas. Members of the two-time world champion Los Angeles Sparks, that city's women's team, garner as much "show time," as their players might say, on any given game day in the plush downtown Staples Center as the men who play for the Lakers, the National Basketball Association (NBA) team that sponsors the Sparks. "When you walk into Madison Square Garden to see the New York Liberty, you take a step back and say, 'this is women's professional basketball!'" Stringer said of New York's WNBA entry. "There are just some things I could not have envisioned." There are undeniable success stories behind the myriad statistics. For instance, it was rowing—not basketball, soccer, or softball—that first propelled women to an unprecedented status at the NCAA level. In January 1996, the NCAA elevated its women's rowing division to championship status, but did not do the same for the men. That decision meant not only that the NCAA agreed to fund the sport's national championship, but also that rowing—historically enjoying strong participation by both men and women—only has NCAA sanction and championship status for its women's crews.

Nikki Franke is living proof of the quieter successes that are telling in their lasting impact. Franke, a former Olympian and the long time coach of the renowned fencing program at Temple University in Philadelphia, traces the growth of her women's team directly to Title IX. In 1972, the year Title IX went into effect, the school elevated fencing from the club level to a team sport for women. "There were no scholarships at the time, but they had a team," Franke said. "That's how it all started." Today, she observes, with all the status her squad has achieved, there are "walk-ons," young women with no history of competition at secondary school levels. And they are accepted, just as they are on men's teams. "If a lady wants to work hard and learn," Franke notes, 'we will work with her."

Claire Smith is assistant sports editor of the Philadelphia Inquirer in Philadelphia, Pennsylvania.

The logo for the Women's professional football league has what appears to be a "Fire bird!" and this sparked my research for this chapter... Because Women MVP's have many of the great traits of this mythical creature, and here in CHAPTER ONE, with the "obstacle to overcome" being EGO... girls, EGO, Hummm, isn't that (the infamous problem everyone else has!)

Well if it's "Them against Us, let's take a peek, at some definitions of EGO from:

/www.cla.purdue.edu/english/theory/psychoanalysis/definitions/superego.html

EGO: For Freud, the ego is "the representative of the outer world to the id" ("Ego and the Id" 708). In other words, the ego represents and enforces the reality-principle whereas the id is concerned only with the pleasure-principle. Whereas the ego is oriented towards perceptions in the real world, the id is oriented towards internal instincts; whereas the ego is associated with reason and sanity, the id belongs to the passions. The ego, however, is never able fully to distinguish itself from the id, of which the ego is, in fact, a part, which is why in his pictorial representation of the mind Freud does not provide a hard separation between the ego and the id. The ego could also be said to be a defense against the superego and its ability to drive the individual subject towards inaction or suicide as a result of crippling guilt. Freud sometimes represents the ego as continually struggling to defend itself from three dangers or masters: "from the external world, from the libido of the id, and from the severity of the super-ego" ("Ego and the Id" 716).

Or masters: "from the external world, from the libido of the id, and from the severity of the super-ego" ("Ego and the Id" 716).

SUPER-EGO: The super-ego is the faculty that seeks to police what it deems unacceptable desires; it represents all moral restrictions and is the "advocate of a striving towards perfection" ("New Introductory Lectures" 22.67). Originally, the super-ego had the task of repressing the Oedipus complex and, so, is closely caught up in the psychodramas of the id; it is, in fact, a reaction-formation against the primitive object-choices of the id, specifically those connected with the Oedipus complex. The young heterosexual male deals with the Oedipus complex by identifying with and internalizing the father and his prohibitions: "The super-ego retains the character of the father, while the more intense the Oedipus complex was and the more rapidly it succumbed to repression (under the influence of discipline, religious teaching, schooling and reading), the more exacting later on is the domination of the super-ego over the ego—in the form of conscience or perhaps of an unconscious sense of guilt" ("Ego and the Id" 706). Given its intimate connection with the Oedipus complex, the super-ego is associated with the dread of castration. As we grow into adulthood, various other individuals or organizations will take over the place of the father and his prohibitions (the church, the law, the police, the government). Because of its connection to the id, the superego has the ability to become *excessively* moral and thus lead to destructive effects. The super-ego is closely connected to the "ego ideal."

And Now:

This history from the Free Dictionary is most revealing for our Woman MVP Training "EGO" work—

From:

http://encyclopedia.thefreedictionary.com/Women%27s+Profes
sional+Football+League

History

In the United States of America, a women's football league was started in the early 1960's. Such an organization was started to prove that women had the power to do what men did, with hopes that people would enjoy women's football as much as they do men's. The name became WPFL in 1965. Since there was no college women's team in the US, most of their athletes came from basketball, rugby, and soccer. In the early 60's, many women thought that sports in the US were sexist and needed a shift in another direction, moving beyond the stereotype that all women were passive. After a few years, the sport began to fade. The league was regenerated in 1998 and has grown stronger every year.

Effects

Sixteen teams in the WPFL are coming into the 2005 season. The league has hundreds of players and is growing, though these female "professional" athletes do not earn any money the league still refers to them as professional athletes. Other leagues that connect to women's football include the United Football League, the Independent Women's Football League, and the Western States Football League. Due to the efforts of these organizations, some women's teams are allowed to play in some of the million-dollar domes and arenas originally built for men's teams. Some of the best places in the world are now hosting women's game like the Astrodome in Houston, Texas, and some of the high facilitated places in Detroit, Michigan.

Meet the Teams

American Conference

Arizona Caliente
Dallas Diamonds
Georgia Gladiators
Houston Energy
Long Beach Aftershock
Los Angeles Amazons
New Mexico Burn
San Francisco Stingrays
So Cal Scorpions

National Conference

Albany Ambush
Cape Fear Thunder
Delaware Griffins
Empire State Roar
Indiana Speed
Minnesota Vixen
New York Dazzles
North Carolina Queens
Northern Ice
Toledo Reign

COACH'S CORNER:

Let's take some coaching tips from a LOGO favorite a "mythical bird" that overcame a (burning desire) type "chick" ego and was reborn to reach greatness...

Hot off the WPFL Logo Now –please, ladies and gentlemen let's "Give it up" for

The Phoenix Bird
(P.S. this is also the logo on my kid's school team)
by Hans Christian Andersen

In the Garden of Paradise,
beneath the Tree of Knowledge,
bloomed a rose bush.
Here, in the first rose, a bird was born.
His flight was like the flashing of light,
his plumage was beauteous,
and his song ravishing.
But when Eve plucked the fruit of the tree
of knowledge of good and evil,
when she and Adam
were driven from Paradise,
there fell from the flaming sword of the cherub
a spark into the nest of the bird,
which blazed up forthwith.
The bird perished in the flames;
but from the red egg in the nest
there fluttered aloft a new one
the one solitary Phoenix bird.
The fable tells that he dwells in Arabia,
and that every hundred years,
he burns himself to death in his nest;
But each time a new Phoenix,
the only one in the world,
rises up from the red egg.
The bird flutters round us,
swift as light,

beauteous in color,
charming in song.
When a mother sits by her infant's cradle,
he stands on the pillow,
and, with his wings,
forms a glory around the infant's head.
He flies through the chamber of content,
and brings sunshine into it,
and the violets on the humble table
smell doubly sweet.

But the Phoenix is not the bird of
Arabia alone.
He wings his way in the glimmer
of the Northern Lights
over the plains of Lapland,
and hops among the yellow flowers
in the short Greenland summer.
Beneath the copper mountains of Fablun,
and England's coal mines, he flies,
in the shape of a dusty moth,
over the hymnbook
that rests on the knees of the pious miner.
On a lotus leaf he floats
down the sacred waters of the Ganges,
and the eye of the Hindu maid
gleams bright when she beholds him.
The Phoenix bird, dost thou not know him?
The Bird of Paradise,
the holy swan of song!
On the car of Thespis he sat

in the guise of a chattering raven,
and flapped his black wings,
smeared with the lees of wine;
over the sounding harp of Iceland
swept the swan's red beak;
on Shakespeare's shoulder he sat
in the guise of Odin's raven,
and whispered in the poet's ear
"Immortality!"
and at the minstrels' feast he fluttered
through the halls of the Wartburg.
The Phoenix bird, dost thou not know him?
He sang to thee the Marseillaise,
and thou kissedst the pen
that fell from his wing;
he came in the radiance of Paradise,
and perchance
thou didst turn away from him,
towards the sparrow who sat
with tinsel on his wings.

The Bird of Paradise,
renewed each century
born in flame,
ending in flame!
Thy picture,
in a golden frame,
hangs in the halls of the rich,
but thou thyself often fliest around,
lonely and disregarded,
a myth—

"The Phoenix of Arabia."
In Paradise,
when thou wert born in the first rose,
beneath the Tree of Knowledge,
thou receivedst a kiss,
and thy right name was given thee
—thy name Poetry...

So this "Bird" coach has a definite message I can feel right off the "bat." It goes something like this- If ya can't take the heat... you know the rest..., burn BABY burn!

COACH'S CORNER:

Take a Look at team logos, and logos of the leagues or the Olympics, even flags.

"Why do you think these particular images were chosen... and How about those mascots...

Life of the party sorts, what is that all about...?

Just marketing and sales, no other meaning to mascots you say?

Well you will have to answer that... for yourself, later, read on.

Let's get pushy, Physical, make contact, no, not yet... instead...Let's put our mental toughness to the test!

Mental Toughness

Softball is different from other sports in that it requires great levels of mental toughness. There is added pressure when one is at bat and while on the field, so a player that is capable to deal with these extra pressures will be successful.

From: www.nationmaster.com/encyclopedia/Softball

It can be hard to imagine "making the team" with all of the stiff competition you'll come up against in your life. There are a lot of people vying for the same spot on the team as you, and these people are bigger, faster, smarter—just plain better than you. Or are they?

Are they really bigger, faster, smarter, better than you? Or is that how you perceive them to be?

COACH'S CORNER:

Let's ask ourselves a few tough questions. Don't be shy to be completely honest in the following pages. This is your living journal, something to mark your accomplishments, learn from your failures and grow into a winning game plan. This is your place to spill it!

• What is your single biggest regret so far in life? Why?

• The cruel thing about regret is that the fault is ours to live with. How did you talk yourself into the decision you made? Why did you choose to make the decision you did?

• Could things have gone differently if you had maintained your mental toughness, and kept your eye on the ball?

• Looking back, how would you do things differently if the same decision presented itself again?

Perhaps Henry Ford said it best. *"If you think you can do a thing or think you can't do a thing, you're right."*

It is amazing what the human mind can do. You and you alone, have the power to fall to defeat or rise to victory.

Many stories of exceptional mental toughness surfaced during the 1988 Olympics in Seoul, South Korea. Among them was the tale of Greg Louganis. The American diver was leading the pack going into his ninth of eleven dives in the 3-metre springboard preliminaries. Attempting a reverse two-and-a-half somersault pike, he hit his head on the board and fell into the water. The dive received a zero.

Louganis' head was stitched with temporary sutures and 35 minutes later, he resumed diving and finished the preliminaries with perfect dives. A trip to the hospital and five mattress stitches later, Louganis returned to the pool the next day and nailed eleven dives to win the Olympic gold medal. A week later, he hit a reverse three-and-a-half somersault off the platform to come from behind and win gold in the platform diving event as well.

Sounds pretty impressive, right?

Now, I'm not an Olympic diver by any stretch but I did have a diving injury when I was in my early 20s. I dove into the lake near our home and went headfirst into a log, splitting my head wide open. I received mega-stitches to close the wound and years later, had to undergo more surgery to remove pieces of wood and scar tissue from my scalp. (Fortunately, my days as a salon owner were put to good use when it came down to styling my hair just right!) I still remember quite vividly how that injury felt and I certainly know I was not interested in diving for a long time afterward!

It's easy to self-doubt but don't let that affect what you know you are capable of—or even things you never thought you were capable of!

COACH'S CORNER:

- **What skills do you possess that could help you achieve your goal? List them, and explain why they are important.**
- **What skills do you not have that would be beneficial to have? List them, and explain why they would be important.**

- Do you want to gain these skills? How can you gain the skills that you don't possess?
- Expose yourself. Is there a hidden talent you have never shown? Why not? What if you could wave a magic wand and see your gift(s) come to life? What was it? How did you discover it?
- If there are hidden talents you've found before, do you believe you possess more?

Mental toughness can be hard to develop because the only real opponent is you. If you choose to doubt, or become discouraged by failure, you can seal your own fate.

So how did Louganis win double gold? He drew on strength you can't find at the gym. He knew what he was capable of, he had no intention of giving up on his Olympic dream and he stayed focus on the goal. He thought he could do something, and he was right.

COACH'S CORNER:

- Have you ever been through an experience where you've displayed great mental toughness? Describe the experience. How did you stay committed to your goal? How did you feel?
- List some of the ways you can keep yourself mentally tough, and focused on your goal. Maybe it's writing your dream down on sticky notes, and posting them around your home as a reminder. Perhaps it's sharing your goal with a trusted friend and turning to them for support when you feel down. There are lots of ways to exercise mental toughness—be creative!
- Keep track of your success! Take a moment now, to make a mental note of times that you've exercised mental

toughness. What was the situation? How did you stay focused on the goal? How did it make you feel?

You need to work hard at tuning out the negative voices in your head telling you that you can't achieve your goal. Whether we are aware of it or not, each one of us has a personal team that governs our lives. This team controls the decisions we make, the actions we take, the thoughts we think. We have the power to cut, sign or keep any or all members of our team at any time.

When we worry, fear or doubt, we give our team members free run of our lives. They jump into the huddle and they make their opinions heard loud and clear until we finally just grab one of their suggestions and go with it. Often with reservations, we choose to ignore our own instincts. That's when you find yourself left bruised and battered in the field, trampled by consequence.

So do we really want to take the suggestions of the likes of these characters?

The key to winning in life is drafting your own team, or league for that matter!

All it takes is three easy steps.
1. Take a good look at your behavior. Be honest with yourself.
2. Identify the players. Get clear on who they are and get to know them one by one. What do they look like? What kinds of things do they contribute to the team?
3. Now decide who on your team can stay and who must be cut. Set them free and remember—you are in charge of your own team and you decide its future direction.

Make sure the team you've chosen is one you want to live with—one you can trust to make solid, sound decisions, and one who won't let life tackle you and drag you down. Choose one member that best exemplifies the theme of each chapter in this book for your winning team. Look at your own circle of people when choosing new team members—you'd be surprised at the positive energy you can find in those closest to you. Or add someone you look up to, who inspires you to achieve your particular goal.

The first member I added to my winning "Wonder Woman," team was Marilyn Tam, a woman (Up from the Ashes and then some!)

To me her story epitomizes the meaning of mental toughness, and rebirth. She has truly kept her eye on the ball, remaining focused on her goal even when life threw a few (very large!) obstacles in her way.

She believes the key to breaking down obstacles and winning the game is mental toughness and inner strength. To attain it, you must always keep your eye on your mission and believe in yourself and the power of Spirit.

Growing up in Hong Kong, Marilyn was told she would never amount to anything because of her gender - common in China where families favor sons. Being the second girl in the family to be followed quickly by three boys made her lot an even more difficult one. Marilyn refused to believe that she was worthless. She found support and solace by anchoring her resolve in Spirit and inner wisdom. She was determined to make a positive difference in the world.

Without her parents' knowledge, she applied for an accelerated program at a co-ed high school that offered a better education than the girls' school she was attending. She was accepted. After two years with her good SAT scores, she left the high school in 10th grade for the United States, alone, for college.

Since then, she has successfully risen to be the Vice President of Nike Apparel and Accessories, President of Reebok Apparel

35

Products and Retail Group and CEO of Aveda. She established the Us Foundation, to collaborate with other organizations to make a positive difference in the world.

Marilyn now travels around the globe working with Fortune 500 companies and non-profit organizations, to speak to and train them on leadership, change management, diversity and community service.

She has attained a life beyond her wildest dreams. She has succeeded in business and in giving back to the world. Most of all, Marilyn is at peace inside. Her recent book, *How to Use What You've Got to Get What You Want,* shares the secrets and discusses the basic tenets of her success: passion, telling the truth, making allies to help you achieve your goals, take risks, make only big mistakes and hold on to your deep convictions.

Not bad for a girl who wasn't supposed to amount to anything!

So now, back to the Phoenix (Fire Bird) for a moment:

Unlike us human folk, The Phoenix is a mythical bird that never dies, the phoenix flies far ahead to the front, always scanning the landscape and distant space. It represents our capacity for vision, for collecting sensory information about our environment and the events unfolding within it. But just like a Woman MVP, the phoenix, with its great beauty, creates intense excitement and deathless inspiration."

In my "spring training" for this chapter I visited many libraries, websites and "read, read, read"... much info on this fascinating Fire bird.... gathering a "world wide" coach's corner - "nest full" - of beautiful tidbits to share with Women MVP's everywhere!

Here we GO!

First Inning - Batter UP!

First in the line up is:

Phoenix (mythology)

From Wikipedia, the free encyclopedia

The phoenix from the Aberdeen Bestiary

For other mythic firebirds, sometimes conflated with the phoenix, see Fire bird (mythology).

In ancient Egyptian mythology and in myths derived from it, the phoenix is a mythical sacred firebird. Said to live for 500, 1461 or for 0(because they are not real) years (depending on the source), the phoenix is a male bird with beautiful gold and red plumage. At the end of its life-cycle the phoenix builds itself a nest of cinnamon twigs that it then ignites; both nest and bird burn fiercely and are reduced to ashes, from which a new, young phoenix arises. The new phoenix embalms the ashes of the old phoenix in an egg made of myrrh and deposits it in Heliopolis ("the city of the sun" in Greek), located in Egypt. The bird was also said to regenerate when hurt or wounded by a foe, thus being almost immortal and invincible — a symbol of fire and divinity.

Although descriptions (and life-span) vary, the phoenix became popular in early Christian art and literature as a symbol of the resurrection, of immortality, and of life-after-death.

Originally, the phoenix was identified by the Egyptians as a stork or heron-like bird called a *benu,* (see Bennu), known from the *Book of the Dead* and other Egyptian texts as one of the sacred symbols of worship at Heliopolis, closely associated with the rising sun and the Egyptian sun-god Ra.

As Britannica 1911 continues:

... Whence it is represented as "self-generating" and called "the soul of Ra (the sun),"—"the heart of the renewed Sun". All the mystic symbolism of the morning sun, especially in connection with the doctrine of the future life, could thus be transferred to the *benu*, and the language of the hymns in which the Egyptians praised the luminary of the dawn as he drew near from Arabia, delighting the gods with his fragrance and rising from the sinking flames of the morning glow, was enough to suggest most of the traits materialized in the classical pictures of the phoenix.

The Greeks adapted the word *benu* (and also took over its further Egyptian meaning of date palm tree), and identified it with their own word *phoinix*, meaning the color purple-red or crimson (of *Phoenicia*). They and the Romans subsequently pictured the bird more like a peacock or an eagle. According to the Greeks the phoenix lived in Arabia next to a well. At dawn, it bathed in the water of the well, and the Greek sun-god Apollo stopped his chariot (the sun) in order to listen to its song.

This myth is famously referred to in Shakespeare's play *The Tempest*, now I will believe that there are unicorns; that in Arabia there is one tree, the phoenix' throne; one phoenix at this hour reigning there - (III.III.27).

One inspiration that has been suggested for the Egyptian phoenix is a specific bird species of East Africa. This bird nests on salt flats that are too hot for its eggs or chicks to survive; it builds a mound several inches tall and large enough to support its egg, which it lays in that marginally cooler location. The convection currents around these mounds resemble the turbulence of a flame. In Russian folklore, the phoenix appears as the Firebird , or firebird, subject of the famous 1910 ballet score by Stravinsky.

The phoenix featured in the flags of Alexander Ypsilantis and of many other captains during the Greek Revolution, symbolizing Greece's rebirth, and was chosen by John Capodistria as the first Coat of Arms of the Greek State (1828-1832). In addition, the first Modern Greek currency bore the name of *phoenix*. Despite being replaced by a royal Coat of Arms, it remained a popular symbol, and was used again in the 1930s by the Second Hellenic Republic. However, its use by the military junta of 1967-1974 made it extremely unpopular, and it has almost disappeared from use after 1974, with the notable exception of the Order of the Phoenix.

The phoenix appears also on the city flags and seals of both Atlanta (torched in the US Civil War) and San Francisco (destroyed by earthquake and fire in 1906) to symbolize their respective rebirths from the ashes.

So in the true tradition of impressing, and great beauty and good works the Women MVP's arise and "take flight," like Tennis Great and founder of the Women's Sports Foundation Billie Jean King when she presented an award to New York Sharks owner Andrea Douglas at the 26th annual Salute to Women in Sports award dinner! It was the Yolanda L. Jackson GiveBack Award!

I can hear it now! The crowd goes wild as The Women MVP Firebirds take to the field! And now-

The New York Sharks have made it to the Pro Football Hall of Fame!

A display of the hall's latest acquisitions includes an IWFL Football signed by the 2005 New York Sharks; it is on display along with items by Pete Rozelle, Walter Payton, Bart Starr and Franco Harris!

This is the FIRST item from a women's football team to be displayed in the Hall of Fame!

COACH'S CORNER:

Take a close look at the LOGOS and "Wild Weather," or CREATURES used to describe some of your favorite teams...

Write them down, and take a good look at the why-when and where you think they may have been chosen, and how that makes you feel both in the Game Zone, and out of it!

Start a scrap book if you prefer, and "look them over!"

Include some of the opposing teams as well... is it the Lions against the Rattlers, or is it the Coyotes against the Ducks?

Have fun with this, and get in the spirit...

You could design your own logo for your team... and give it a name NOW... and get into the "team spirit!"

Even make up your own character or name and just play away!

CHAPTER TWO
IN THE BIG LEAGUES

Obstacle to overcome: FEAR

M — (My)

The only thing we have to fear is fear itself - nameless, unreasoning, unjustified, terror which paralyzes needed efforts to convert retreat into advance."

–FDR - First Inaugural Address, March 4, 1933

V — (Victory)

"What are fears but voices airy?
Whispering harm where harm is not.
And deluding the unwary
Till the fatal bolt is shot!"

–Wordsworth

P — (Plan)

Courage is not the lack of fear but the ability to face it.
–Lt. John B. Putnam Jr.

- be afraid or feel anxious or apprehensive about a possible or probable situation or event; "I fear she might get aggressive"

41

- be afraid or scared of; be frightened of; "I fear the winters in Moscow"; "We should not fear the Communists!"
- an emotion experienced in anticipation of some specific pain or danger (usually accompanied by a desire to flee or fight)
- be sorry; used to introduce an unpleasant statement; "I fear I won't make it to your wedding party"
- concern: an anxious feeling; "care had aged him"; "they hushed it up out of fear of public reaction"
- be uneasy or apprehensive about; "I fear the results of the final exams"
- reverence: regard with feelings of respect and reverence; consider hallowed or exalted or be in awe of; "Fear God as your father"; "We venerate genius"
- a profound emotion inspired by a deity; "the fear of God" wordnet.princeton.edu/perl/webwn

So what is everyone afraid of?

How does a Woman MVP in training identify the line so it isn't crossed?

Research shows that men often compete harder than women because their attitudes toward competition are different. Men are work-centered, likely to negotiate and likely to ask for better treatment. Many women are trained from childhood to be people pleasers. They don't want to appear pushy or put strain on an employee-employer relationship, and tend to be passive in their business dealings.

A lot of women compensate for this by becoming overly aggressive. The key is recognizing the difference between being assertive and being aggressive. Being assertive means speaking up or saying no with respect. Being aggressive is acting with contempt for the other people involved. Assertive women feel stronger and more relaxed about their work while aggressive women create feelings of frustrations and stress that affect work performance negatively.

Let's look at some "fear based" approaches:

Offence verses defense... or in other words...

Assertive vs. Aggressive

There is a fine line between being assertive and being aggressive and a woman needs to know the difference. I hate to say it, but labels still exist. Have you ever seen an aggressive businessman called a bitch? No! He's probably called the CEO. I recently received an e-mail that illustrates what I'm talking about.

The basic difference between being assertive and being aggressive is how our words and behavior affect the rights and well being of others.

–"Wonder Woman" Sharon Anthony

We have heard many versions of the Pros and their approaches... I like to (tongue in cheek) ponder this one...

How to Tell a Businessman from a Businesswoman

A businessman is aggressive; a businesswoman is pushy.

A businessman is good on details; she is picky.

He loses his temper because he's so involved in his job; she is bitchy.

When he is depressed (or hung-over), everyone tiptoes past his office; she is moody, so it must be her time of the month.

He follows through; she doesn't know when to quit.

He's confident; she's conceited.

He stands firm; she's impossible to deal with.

He is firm; she is hard.

His judgments are her prejudices.

He drinks because of the excessive job pressure; she's a lush.

He isn't afraid to say what he thinks; she's mouthy.

He's close-mouthed; she's secretive.

He climbed the ladder to success; she slept her way to the top.

He is a stern taskmaster; she's hard to work for.

He is witty; she is sarcastic.

Author unknown

COACH'S CORNER:

Let's start out with a simple exercise.

- **Define "assertive" List examples of assertive behavior.**
- **Define "aggressive" List examples of aggressive behavior.**
- **Now read your definitions. Are they similar, or very different from each other? Are the behaviors or actions you've listed similar or different?**

I whipped out my trusted Merriam-Webster Dictionary and took a peek at their definitions. To assert one, according to them, is "to declare or state positively." To show aggression is "a forceful action or procedure (as an unprovoked attack) especially when intended to dominate or master." Interestingly enough, they've listed these words as synonyms of each other.

I have to say I disagree. To me, there is a big difference between each of these words. To me, assertion is firmly stating what you believe or know to be true with respect to other people. Aggression is intimidating others to have them do what you want, or to force an opinion on them. These hardly seem to be interchangeable words! Anyone who has ever dealt with an aggressor will tell you that there is a difference between the two, and they can probably also tell you how they'd rather be treated.

There will be times in your life when you have to convince people why they should believe in you and your dream. An example would be going to the bank for a loan to start your small business. They will question you—even challenge you—so it's up to you how you want to present your case. Do you state the facts and explain logically why you believe in this particular goal, and how you will take steps to achieve it? Or do you resort to scare tactics and force your opinion on them by raising your voice, attacking their questions (or them personally—"You're not a jeweler, what the hell do you know about opening a jewelry store?") or giving them ultimatums? If the cleat were on the other foot, so to speak, how would you like to be treated?

I can't imagine going on when there are no more expectations.
    –"Wonder Woman" Dame Edith Evans

I was in one of my favorite stores the other day, waiting in line to exchange a shirt that was the wrong size (teenage boys—how they grow so fast!) A large man in front of me was trying to return a pair of pants without tags or a receipt. The store's employee, a petite young woman, was explaining to this gentleman that store policy dictates no refunds are given for items that come without tags or a receipt. By this time, the man was quite agitated (scared of something maybe?) and he loudly told the employee that he did not—and never would—shop in this store, and he simply wanted his money back (even though it was a gift) so he could buy something he really wanted. Again, the young woman explained in an apologetic tone that she was not authorized to refund the money without tags or a receipt. Red in the face, this man put his hands on the counter and leaned in so he towered over the employee. "If you don't refund me immediately, I will speak to your manager and have

45

you fired. (a real Goliath type) I will also make sure that everyone I talk to knows about the poor service in this place, he continued." I have to give the girl credit. She stood her ground, looked at this raging man in front of her and said, "I will gladly give you the name of my manager, but I will not be refunding your money today, sir."

Well, I thought this guy was going to blow a gasket! After a few more threats, he finally stormed away—without his refund. I made my exchange and on the way home, I thought about the scene I had witnessed. Had this man kept a cool head, I'm sure he could have struck a deal with the employee. While he wouldn't have gotten a refund, he could have perhaps gotten store credit that one of his friends or family could use (since he didn't shop there!) Or perhaps had he pleaded his case with honey, not vinegar, he could have talked her into a partial refund and recovered some money.

I understand that sometimes it is hard to draw the line, and not fall over onto the "aggressive" side but take a step back and look at the situation again before acting. This is a good time to learn from example!

COACH'S CORNER:

- Have you ever been on the receiving end of an aggressor's rant? Describe the situation.
- Did it frighten you? What aggressive behaviors did this person display? Were you filled with fear? How did it make you feel?
- What was the outcome of the situation? Could things have gone differently if the aggressor had just been assertive?
- Have you ever been the aggressor? Explain the situation. Why did you act the way that you did? How did it make you feel?

- **What ways could you have handled the situation differently?**

Sport, especially the full-contact variety such as football and hockey, is a great example of the blurred line between aggression and assertion. Where do athletes draw the line between what is part of the game and what is simply violent aggression, and what if in the "heat" of it all they simply "lose it!"

Scary thought?

Here's an example of a player who could really "stick handle" his way around and out...

On March 8, 2004, Todd Bertuzzi of the NHL's Vancouver Canucks sucker-punched Colorado Avalanche rookie Steve Moore from behind, knocking Moore to the ground. Bertuzzi fell on top of Moore, and drove his face into the ice when they landed. What should be mentioned is that footage of the incident showed Bertuzzi stalking Moore around the ice before the attack. It left Moore with three broken vertebrae, nerve damage and a concussion.

The attack stemmed from an earlier playoff game in February where Moore laid an open-ice shoulder hit to Vancouver's captain Marcus Nasland that left the star player unconscious and later, out of a playoff game with a concussion. No call was made on the hit by the referees or the league upon review. After the game, a few Vancouver players made it clear that there was a bounty on Moore's head.

Bertuzzi was fined, suspended for the rest of the playoffs and had to apply for reinstatement for the 2006 season. (The 2005 season was a wash due to stalled contract negotiations.) Despite protests from NHL Commissioner Gary Bettman, who said the league had punished Bertuzzi enough, the Vancouver police charged him with criminal assault, which he plead guilty to in return for conditional discharge with no criminal record.

And Moore—His career is most likely finished. He filed a civil suit against Bertuzzi, the Vancouver Canucks and several players from the team. He's undergoing severe physical rehab but the Colorado Avalanche did not renew his contract at the end of the 2004 season.

COACH'S CORNER:

Let's pretend for a moment. Let's pretend that you are walking down the street, minding your own business when a woman, slightly larger than you, approaches and tries to instigate a fight. You recognize her as the woman at the supermarket who accused you of butting in line ahead of her. You refuse. You turn your back and start walking away when she punches you in the head. As you—knocked unconscious—fall to the ground, this same woman jumps on your back and slams your face into the asphalt. You wake up in the hospital with three broken vertebrae, nerve damage and a concussion.

What do you suppose would happen?

I'm guessing by the time you wake up in the hospital, the attacker would have already been arrested and charged with aggravated assault.

But in the case of athlete "enforcer" Todd Bertuzzi, he was suspended from his job for what little was left of the season, given a small fine when you consider his salary and didn't spend one second anywhere near a jail. What are worse, people seem upset that Moore hasn't been a sport and offered Bertuzzi his forgiveness. No, instead he's brought a civil suit against the poor guy. What kind of sportsmanship is that?

There seems to be a high tolerance for violence in sports. Intimidation and fear based, or passionate "win at all costs," aggression is simply accepted, if not encouraged. Does this translate off the ice?

Do people need to be aggressive to do well in business?

More importantly, do people always know when they've become aggressive?

Most athletes will tell you that they don't focus on anything other than winning. They don't see their opponents as real people but merely obstacles that they must go around...or through. I suppose some, could say the same for business. When negotiating contracts, you don't normally look across the boardroom table and see a father, or a wife, a son, daughter or a sister or brother.

You see someone you need to persuade to agree with you on an issue.

The best way to persuade someone certainly isn't to intimidate or threaten, to plant FEAR. All this really does is to create resentment, even if you succeed in getting what you want. Eventually, this is just going to come around and boot you in the butt. Coercion might work in one instance but cause ongoing resentment in others people do often have "good memories" even of "bad or unpleasant" times they would rather forget.

You never know who will be your boss, or whose help you may need much later down the road.

Burning bridges is tricky stuff, indeed.

Trying to control a person doesn't work either. Any parent will know that as soon as you tell your child to do something, they often do the complete opposite, reverse psychology is often a better choice.

Or, as soon as you tell someone NOT to do something, guess what? It doesn't change as you get older. As soon as someone tells me that I can't do something—whether they don't think I'm capable or I'm just not allowed—that just lights a fire in me. It's kind of

49

an "I'll show them!" spirit, I've heard that is true of many, and has actually inspired some of the planets most amazing works!

I have dealt with a lot of people in my life—all different kinds, including my own children. In my limited experience I've found there's only one way to persuade any one, truthfully, I must respect them, and they respect me.

Don't try to belittle them or tell them they're wrong in an attempt to shine the light on your ideas and ways.

Listen to them without interrupting (I always tell my kids that I hate when they keep talking when I'm interrupting!) with a reason why your idea is so much better, give them some sugar (remember, you catch more bees with honey than with vinegar), provide options for them to choose from, give them the benefits of choosing your option and support them no matter what they decide to do…even if it's not agreeing with you, (you can learn a few things too, from this exercise!)

They will respect you in return and you might find it easier to persuade them the next time you meet, or even in this round.

Let's try this out in an exercise!

Now let's meet an all time GREAT!

Babe Didrikson Zaharias

"All of my life I have always had the urge to do things better than anybody else."

–Babe Didrikson Zaharias

Babe Didrickson Zaharias first came into national prominence as a basketball player. Though but a teen-ager, she was nominated for three All-American teams and once scored 106 points in a game. Of the 634 track and field events in which she was entered, she won all but 12. She also excelled at golf, winning the U.S. Amateur title in 1946, the British Amateur in 1947 and the Women's professional titles in 1948, 1950, and 1954. In baseball, she toured the country with a team composed mostly of men and could throw a ball 300 feet on a straight line. (She also threw a third strike past Joe DiMaggio.) In bowling, she rolled a 237 game and averaged 170. (Source: *The Great American Sports Book* by George Gipe, Doubleday & Company, Inc., New York)

Jim Murray, *LA Times* sportswriter, described her thus: "She was brave as a lion, as lovable as a lamb. She bragged, she swore, drank, but could be presented at court, comfort a nun, buy a fur for her mother or sew a dress for her as well as the product of any finishing school. She was a roughneck with a basketball or a deck of cards in her hands. But she grew roses, raised poodles, danced at the White House and hung curtains like the dutiful Scandinavian housewife she was."

That babe was—No Scardy Cat!

There are more MVP's also who were not afraid to step out on a limb, Please, Meet Debi Rolfing, ANOTHER ALL TIME GREAT on the "playing field of Life!"

She took to the field and "Passed some winning plays on the business and personal front!"

This EXERPT from Debi's website... is a "telling tale!"
www.debirolfing.com

Their long list of projects includes the development of The Plantation at Kapalua resort on Maui. The Plantation includes a world-class golf course, plantation style clubhouse and a residential real estate project.

Debi has been a top producer in real estate sales on Maui for many years and heads up their charitable foundation, while sitting on the boards of other local charities.

Mark produces his own golf show Golf Hawaii with Mark Rolfing, aired on The Golf Channel. He is also a golf commentator for NBC Sports.

Debi and Mark's most recent project deals with something on a "smaller" scale and that is newborn babies. The couple is registered to accept infants into foster care in Montana and Hawaii while babies are awaiting adoption.

Whether the project is large or small, Debi and her husband Mark do it in a big way.

After a twenty-nine year career as a real estate broker and developer, Debi Rolfing's life has traveled full circle back to a simpler, purer stage that she cherished as a preschool teacher at Holy Innocence when she first arrived on Maui in 1976. Today Debi is dedicated to her volunteer work as a licensed foster mother with the same passion that she gave a variety of other successful ventures throughout her career.

In September of 1998, Debi and her husband Mark were licensed by the State of Montana, Department of Public Health and Human Services, as youth foster home parents. While in Montana, they provide "cradle care" home service through Catholic Social Services, Lutheran Social Services and Child & Family Services, State of Montana, for placement of babies, age 0-3 months, as transition care from birth to reunification or relinquishment by the birthmother to the placement with adoptive parents. They have provided foster care for twenty-one (21) newborns. In September of 2001, Debi was asked by the Child and Family Service Agency through the State of Montana to provide foster care to a sweet baby girl born September 11th, the fateful day that the nation was attacked by terrorists and lost thousands of

American family members. This baby girl, affectionately called "Faith," represented the spirit of hope and love that embodies her ministry of foster care.

In the summer of 1999, Debi and Mark were licensed by the State of Hawaii as youth foster home parents. Debi completed 33 hours of P.R.I.D.E. (Parents' Resource for Information, Development and Education) training on Maui. She attended the spring 2000 Session of Foster and Adoptive Parent Training in Kalispell, Montana and the Spring 2002 National Foster Parents Association, Inc. Annual Education Conference in Las Vegas, Nevada. Debi is a graduate of Keeping Children Safe and Families Strong. This certification was completed in spring 2003 in Kalispell, Montana. She annually attends the programs Separation and Loss class to help her with detachment from her newborns after placement.

While in Montana caring for medically fragile newborns, Debi volunteers her expertise through her membership in Montana State Foster/Adoptive Parent Association and Sunburst Community Service Foundation. She has 10,132 volunteer hours in foster care for newborns.

Debi has established a reputation over the past 29 years as one of Maui's most successful real estate brokers. She became active in the real estate profession after moving to Maui in 1976.

With an approved resume of over 100 million dollars of sales in the development of The Plantation at Kapalua project. Numerous awards and record-breaking sales illustrate her organizational skills and marketing sales capabilities.

While working in general brokerage in the 1980's, Debi participated in over 15 million dollars of sale transactions, a

53

record in those days. As a Realtor Associate in 1978 with Stapleton Associates, Lahaina, she was awarded Top Producer-Salesman and Top Producer-Listing Agent in her first year in the real estate profession.

In early 1985, she and husband, Mark, formed Rolfing Productions; a Maui based sports marketing company. The "one-of-its-kind" operation on Maui marketed, televised, produced and organized prominent golf and basketball tournaments for the Valley Isle. Such tournaments as the Kapalua International, Kaanapali Classic, and Maui Classic grew into major sporting events bringing professional sports attracting tourists to Maui. Debi continued to serve on the Executive Committee of the Lincoln-Mercury Kapalua International until the final year in 1997.

Their tournament has grown into the PGA Tour's Season Opening Event, The Mercedes Championship.

Debi's involvement in the planning, development and marketing of The Plantation at Kapalua has contributed to its success today.

The Plantation consists of an award winning Coore & Crenshaw designed 18-hole championship golf course, which plays host to the PGA Tour Season opening Mercedes Championship each January, a Plantation-style 33,000 sq. ft. The Clubhouse and the Plantation Estates encompass 222 acres of residential real estate.

Debi and Mark are recognized as Founders of the Maui Arts & Cultural Center and The Art School at Kapalua, Maui.

Debi is currently on the Board of Directors of Maui Family Support Services and Family Concepts in Kalispell. These organizations are close to her heart. Her primary volunteer focus is to foster newborns in her Maui and Montana homes while they await reunification with their birthparents or adoption.

While traveling with her husband Mark on The PGA Tour, Debi volunteers her time in The PGA Tour Family Center's nursery, caring for the professional's children. Summer of 2003, Debi was honored to be included in the Board of Directors of the FORE Adoption Foundation. The mission of this foundation is to help United States children find permanent loving homes by providing financial support in the form of direct grants to Adoptive Parents for attorney and agency fees, court approved birthmother expenses and an education fund for the adoptive child.

The foundation leaders, professional golfer Kirk Triplett and his wife Cathi, who have the Triplett Tour Fore Adoption, received the "National Angels in Adoption" award in September 2004 from the Congressional Coalition on Adoption Institute.

Debi along with her husband Mark feel honored to have been able to provide volunteer emergency care to 21 medically and in some cases critically fragile newborns over the past six years.

These two winners are definitely on the "Defense" line for many in this life, and how blessed I am to have met Debi in person, "In a hair salon…where else" during the Sony Open! She has a special light, and I have grown to Love her dearly!

Debi has been assertive in a unique way—the former real estate broker has sought and found homes for 21 babies since 1990. Despite phenomenal success in the fast-paced world of real estate, Debi was looking for something more. She found it when she and her husband purchased the Kootenai Lodge property in Montana. Needing something to fill the expansive lodge, Debi was turned to the idea of fostering babies as they awaited adoption. While some were quick to go, Debi had to fight hard to find homes for some "unlovable" babies—primarily those with mental or physical disabilities. Her proudest—and saddest—day was giving away baby Will, a child with Down syndrome, after 74 days.

A Loving heart, a Brave spirit, and a whole series of Winning Plays... How wonderful!

COACH'S CORNER:

What are you doing for your community? How could you join a team effort to contribute to a better world?

Then make the call... do the deed!

CHAPTER THREE
YOU DON'T MAJOR IN THE MINORS

Obstacle to overcome: WRONG IDEAS

M — (My)

The only real mistake is the one from which we learn nothing.
–John Powell

V — (Victory)

If you have an apple and I have an apple and we exchange these apples then you and I will still each have one apple. But if you have an idea and I have an idea and we exchange these ideas, then each of us will have two ideas.

–George Bernard Shaw

P — (Plan)

The best way to have a good idea is to have lots of ideas.
–Linus Pauling

Hey Ladies!
Now come Now, Let's be honest, have you ever gotten an e-

mail like this one below…which is filled with girl locker "get the lead out" coach type room chat, and then followed with a tag line that now you "must" send this off in order to receive…do as I say…and you too can get lucky, kind of jargon!

Well, here is mine, it came to me from a gal that I had not spoken to for quite some time…but I guess she hit send to all…or something, because "silly me" thinking it was an olive branch called this gal right after…and got hung up on!

So, "don't major in the minors" is all about "keeping it REAL! And real focused…make all your moves because they advance you or your mission, don't be a phony, and don't think you deserve to be ordered around either, unless you are doing something you believe in…

My e-mail went something like this…

Prepare yourselves:

Women MVP's Here's comes the "Drill!"

A WOMAN SHOULD HAVE…
> A set of screwdrivers,
> A cordless drill, and
> A black lace bra…

A WOMAN SHOULD HAVE…
> One friend who
> Always makes her
> Laugh…
> And one
> Who lets her cry…?

A WOMAN SHOULD HAVE…
> A good piece of furniture
> Not previously owned
> Anyone else in her family…

A WOMAN SHOULD HAVE...
Eight matching plates,
Wine glasses with stems,
And a recipe for a meal that will
Make her guests feel honored.
A WOMAN SHOULD HAVE...
A feeling of control over her destiny...
EVERY WOMAN SHOULD KNOW...
How to fall in love without losing herself...
EVERY WOMAN SHOULD KNOW...
HOW TO QUIT A JOB
BREAK UP WITH A LOVER
AND CONFRONT A FRIEND WITHOUT RUIN-
ING THE FRIENDSHIP...
EVERY WOMAN SHOULD KNOW...
When to try harder... and
WHEN TO WALK AWAY...
EVERY WOMAN SHOULD KNOW...
That she can't change
The length of her calves,
The width of her hips, or
The nature of her parents...
EVERY WOMAN SHOULD KNOW...
That her childhood
May not have been perfect...
But; It's over...
EVERY WOMAN SHOULD KNOW...
What she would and wouldn't
Do for love or more...
EVERY WOMAN SHOULD KNOW...
How to live alone, Even if she doesn't like it

EVERY WOMAN SHOULD KNOW...
Whom she can trust, whom she can't,
And why she shouldn't take it personally...
EVERY WOMAN SHOULD KNOW...
Where to go...
Be it to her best friend's kitchen table...
Or a charming inn in the woods,
When her soul needs soothing...
EVERY WOMAN SHOULD KNOW...
What she can and can't accomplish
In a day,
A month...
And a year

Take it or leave it, Ladies, these emails and others like them seem to be flooding our "In boxes!"

To give yourself the best possible chance of playing to your potential, you must prepare for every eventuality. That means practice.
                                                        –Steve Ballesteros

So be sure you take what you want from what we are told "Women should Know, Be or Do," make it your own and if the cleat fits... well then... take to the field, girlfriend!

Now that your, "getting the right idea."

Let's focus on Setting Goals...

When my fourteen year old daughter was asked to set one hundred life goals as a homework assignment, she never blinked an eye, but instead she got the idea right away... Humm, she proudly proclaimed as her little fingers danced across the computer keyboard ... Look MOM I did 170, I went the "extra Mile"!

60

I just had to peek over her shoulder and see what kind of goals she wrote, her smile was so filled with Hope and dreamy eyes took over her glance, as she proudly leaned to the left and allowed me in to take a closer look.

They are a "quick read" but here are ALL of my daughter's life goals-At fourteen and completely "un-jaded" let's let the children "coach us a little in this "right idea" coaching exercise.

Could you (Go the extra mile?) Like a child dreaming of the "big future" and all it's possibilities—could you get so excited about this assignment like my daughter Jinji did that you could "power down" over a hundred of these? Yes there's lots, but come on... we are in training here; give them all a read... even if it's just a "quickie!"

Please keep an open mind, and take the lead from a "child coach," and "Aim High!" When you shoot to WIN!

COACH'S CORNER:

Don't skip... anything in this book ... as "irrelevant as it may seem to you, unless you are jumping up and down with a "skipping Rope!" then come back and read it ALL!

Be patient, no matter how grueling, and even silly it can get at times ... it is all important ...Women MVP's stick to the training!

170 Life Goals

By Jinji age fourteen:

1. Visit all 50 states (current count: Arizona, California, Colorado, Georgia, Hawaii, Idaho, Illinois, Indiana, Maryland, Michigan, Montana, Nevada, New York, Ohio, Oregon, Texas, Virginia, Washington, West Virginia, Wyoming)

2. Have my picture taken on top of the Eiffel Tower
3. Read The Hobbit
4. See all 100 movies of the AFI top 100 list
5. Go snorkeling in Hawaii
6. Spend a winter in Vermont
7. Fall in love and get married
8. Have a kid or many (at most two) kids
9. Play craps in Las Vegas
10. Spend a summer in Tahoe
11. Photograph the Grand Canyon in black and white
12. Learn how to sail a boat
13. Learn Chinese
14. Learn how to make laniards
15. Learn how to use a sewing machine* and make a costume
16. Go to England
17. Walk on the Great Wall of China
18. See the Great Barrier Reef
19. Take a tour of the Hershey Factory
20. Be in a movie
21. Become Famous
22. Ride a Husky
23. Take a year off when I am 50
24. And become an old lady
25. Who lives alone in the top apartment with a bunch of cats.
26. Go To Africa and help sick children.
27. Marry Tom Boob-chicken (I just added this one so when My teacher got here he would laugh) because my goal is to make more people laugh whenever I can
28. Have to Identical Twin Girls

29. Help poor impoverished kids in America
30. Meet the President (of the U.S.) and become the first lady President...
31. Graduate from University
32. Get a Masters
33. Get a PhD
34. Go on Jeopardy
35. Eat 20 Muffins on my birthday
36. Stick my face in my birthday cake and eat it
37. Try acupuncture
38. Write a novel
39. Publish a paper
40. Serve at least one term on the Board of Trustees for a school district
41. Visit the site where the twin towers used to be
42. Live in the jungle with Koalas and Pandas for a day
43. Try not to use any gas or electricity for a day
44. Go to Europe
45. Collect all 50 state quarters
46. Plant a garden
47. Go surfing
48. Go sky diving
49. Learn how to make cheese
50. Make a soufflé
51. Cure cancer
52. Learn how to Taiko drum (more than just the workshop)
53. Sell something on Ebay
54. Fly
55. Be O.K. with having a wild and wonderful dream
56. Write a song
57. Buy a laptop

58. Climb a tree
59. Ride in a hot air balloon
60. Go skydiving
61. Learn how to fuse glass
62. Go to the Oregon Zoo
63. Climb a tall mountain so I can lie there and look at the stars
64. Learn Italian
65. Learn how to fish (and catch a fish barehanded)
66. Learn how to ride a horse
67. Read Harry Potter and the Sorcerer's Stone
68. Learn to play the violin (a little bit)
69. Compose a song
70. Learn how to ski better
71. Bake an cinnamon apple pie from scratch
72. Learn to ballroom dance
73. Learn how to pull up a pot on the potter's wheel
74. See Niagara Falls
75. Learn how to make paper (I saw some made from animal dung once)
76. Learn how to do laundry
77. Meet all the people I've ever wanted to meet
78. Do absolutely nothing for a day
79. Learn how to use a lighter
80. Work at Disneyland As the Little Mermaid
81. Join a choir
82. Learn how to play go
83. Make lasagna from scratch
84. Make a sock monkey
85. Go on a road trip
86. Go to the Opera

87. Go to the Symphony
88. Read the newspaper on a regular basis (New York Times online)
89. Vote
90. Make a candle
91. Paint with oil on canvas
92. Roll my own sushi
93. Build my own sandcastle
94. Learn how to juggle
95. Be an incredible athlete in some sport
96. Have a poem published in an anthology
97. Make soap
98. Go paint-balling
99. Go laser tagging
100. Go to the Shakespeare Festival in Ashland
101. Paint a mural in Steele
102. Be in two places at once
103. Play pool
104. Play chess
105. Swim
106. Learn Dream-weaver
107. Learn Adobe Photoshop and Bryce
108. Make crème brule from scratch and use a cooking torch
109. Make mochi from scratch
110. Cook dumplings from scratch
111. See Rocky Horror Picture show at the theatre
112. Become Reed Van certified
113. Pull the handle of a slot machine
114. Baked a double-layer cake
115. Teach summer camp
116. Be Mayor of Anaheim for a day

117. Win a spelling bee, an oral interpretation contest, a writing contest, a music

118. Composition contest, a coloring contest (many!), a poetry contest, an   art contest

119. Learn how to fold a paper crane

120. Memorize the preamble

121. Take ballet and tap

122. Wear a watch all the time

123. Learn how to light a match

124. Learn calligraphy

125. Learn how to make paper

126. Learn how to speak French

127. Learn photography (developing and printing)

128. Learn the airbrush and the potter's wheel

129. Learn to waltz, tango, foxtrot, and swing

130. Be on TV

131. Have my picture in the newspaper on the front page

132. Ride in a taxi, a train, a plane, an omnibus, a tram, a car, a bus, a light rail, or the

133. Subway, the BART, a trolley all in the same day

134. Learn to play flute and piccolo

135. Be music librarian and section leader

136. Be in Girl Scouts

137. Get my Gold Award in something

138. Be in Mock Trial and be team captain

139. Have a French Pen pal

140. Gave a Chinese pen pal, that I write gibberish to and Claim its English.

141. Get my driver's license

142. Go to prom

143. Go to Homecoming

144. Go to the Lotus festival, the Date Festival, the Korean Festival, the Japanese
145. Festival...
146. Be in a marching band
147. Collect all the Aladdin stickers
148. Go snowshoeing
149. Learn to contra dance
150. Learn lindy hop
151. Teach an elementary school class
152. See the Columbia River Gorge
153. See the Portland Rose Gardens
154. Have an ice cream sundae in Ghiradelli Square
155. Climb up to Coit Tower
156. See Miss Saigon
157. Become Miss America
158. Meet David Copperfield
159. Play in an orchestra
160. Visit Fermilab
161. Be at Disneyland, backstage!—go on the special Fantasmic tour :)
162. Learn how to use Mathmatica
163. Learn how to program in Java
164. Teach a Paideia class
165. (dancing with the stars) Waltz in Eliot circle
166. See Litehouse perform
167. See Five for Fighting perform
168. Learn how to play Set! and be good at it
169. Find a cure for Aids
170. COMPLETE ALL MY GOALS!!!

WHEW, You Go Girl!

67

I say why not? …. To my Girl… thumbs Up Baby!
And to you too… Women MVP's are we!
So: How'd you do?
Wanna give it a try?
Come now… How many life goals can you set?
How many have you patted your back for reaching?

COACH'S CORNER:

Let's pause and do it now… Set your own number, do a large number then narrow it down to your top ten if you prefer… but focus, focus, focus …be good at "Laying out a "true to you" Life Wish List"

A solid game plan is the key to competing for women. I am proud to say that even at fourteen my little girl… O.K. little teenager is off to the races!

Time to "Make a plan, Stan" (Probably, short for Stantinopal) don't dismiss, before you understand, please, read on dear woman MVP in training…

In honor of one of my daughter's goals, Learning Italian, here is a "spell,"we can cast about the "numbers game!"

From: www.sacred-texts.com

English nursery song:–

"*Constantinople, stantinople, tinople, nople, ople,* pull!
Pull, ople, nople, tinople, stantinople, Constantinople."

In which we have the counting or addition and subtraction in a different form. The spell or child's game as used in Tuscany is, however, applied to good luck, and runs as follows: Taking ten acorns, the actor sings:–

"Tu lo sai la voglio fare,
Per l'indietro io voglio mandare,
La verita in mia mano la deve dare,
Queste diande per l'indietro io contero
Fino al uno io tornero.
E se mai non sbagliero,
La vittoria io la vincero.
Adesso io incomincio
Da uno, due, tre quattro,
Cinque, sei, sette otto, nove e dieci
Dieci, nove otto, sette,
Sei, cinque, quattro, tre
Due–uno!
Senza mai sbagliare,
La vittoria io la devo fare,
E mai nel contare io sbagliero
La vittoria io vincero."

Or in English:–

"You know what I want to do.
I will work it back for you,
The truth shall be at my command.
I will count these acorns in my hand
There shall no error be.
Thus I'll gain a victory,
And so I now begin, you see:
From one, two, three, four,
Five, six, seven, eight, nine, ten.
Ten, nine, eight, seven,

Six, five, four, three,
Two–one.
So without the least mistake
now the victory I take.
I have counted well and true,
To me the victory is due!"

Number games?

Totally, absorbed attitude stuff...Score boards, possibly, a traditionally male-oriented skill, which women fail to embrace.

Whatever women choose to do in life, whether it's starting a business or advancing their career with a promotion, it is important to develop a game plan that reflects your strategy for winning.

Committing to a goal is not as simple as writing it down.

Include a timeframe and a "scoreboard," for reaching that goal and write down the steps needed to achieve it. First Inning... two down bases are full, and your up to bat.... The pressure is on!

When it comes to business and Life in general, fear may be more of a factor for women than men. Women are more hesitant to take risks that may lead to ultimate success. The interesting thing about a game plan is it reduces the fear factor. The plan provides the security of a mapped out route that women need to get started, and it serves as a guiding force to get you back on track when things go wrong.

Anna Ouroumian, President and CEO of the Academy of Business Leadership, knows all about taking risks. Anna was an orphan in war-torn Beirut and by the time she reached her teens, she knew her only chance at success was in the United States.

Just 17-years-old, Anna took an illegal trip by fishing boat into the Mediterranean and hopped a boat bound for Cyprus. Refugees like her swarmed the US Embassy but Anna had a game plan with a goal. She talked her way past the crowd and boarded a Los Angeles-bound plane with her new visa just a few weeks later.

She graduated at the top of her UCLA class, worked with Ronald Reagan and volunteered at charities. Now, she helps at-risk youth learn about economics by writing their own game plans and interacting with the movers and shakers of corporate America.

We are the music makers, and we are the dreamers of the dream. Wandering by lone sea breakers, and sitting by desolate streams. World losers and world forsakers, for whom the pale moon gleams, yet we are movers and the shakers of the world forever it seems.

–Arthur William Edgar O'Shaughnessy

COACH'S CORNER:

Scoreboards are a Bling bling, thing…. Some leg work, with diamond encrusted ankle bracelets, mandatory—ladies!

Write a solid game plan, and YES, keep score!

Achieving a goal is NOT as simple as writing it down, there is some "elbow grease" required.

As I mention in my Eye of the Tiger Discussion Book, and audio series located at www.eyeofthetiger.us

I read a study that looked at a class of high school graduates—a "where are they now?" sort of thing. Researchers found that those students who physically wrote down their goals were 94% wealthier than their fellow students who didn't. I'm not suggesting that by simply writing down, "I want to be a millionaire by the time I'm 35" is going to make you a millionaire by the time you're 35. You do have to work toward that goal. But by simply writing down a goal, you're committing to it. When you write down a goal, you make that little dream inside your head something that exists in reality.

To respond is positive, to react is negative.

—"Big Boy" Zig Ziglar

COACH'S CORNER:

For example, people trying to lose weight are often told to keep a food diary. A journal like that does many things:

1. It names your goal.

"I will lose 10 pounds by the end of next month."

2. It keeps track of your journey toward that goal, including where you are at a certain time or how far you've come since you began.

"Last month, I weighed 173 pounds. This month, I weigh 161 pounds."

3. It keeps you motivated by reminding you of your successes. "On Monday, I passed on birthday cake at a coworker's party and at my Friday weigh-in, I had lost two pounds!"

4. It tells you where you need improvement by tracking failures. "Today I scarfed down two doughnuts and a tub of French vanilla ice cream—not frozen yogurt and yes, an entire tub."

5. It lets you know of any holes in your plan.

"I don't have a section in my diary to track the amount of exercise I do, so I am going to add one."

The more we are able to give definition to our dreams, the clearer they become and the better our connection to the positive forces that can support our dream becoming a reality.

CHAPTER FOUR
SEASON TRAINING

Obstacle to overcome: NEGATIVE SELF IMAGE

M — (My)

First say to yourself what you would be; and then do what you have to do.

–Epictetus

V — (Victory)

A strong, positive self-image is the best possible preparation for success.

–"Wonder Woman" Joyce Brothers

P — (Plan)

The "self-image" is the key to human personality and human behavior. Change the self image and you change the personality and the behavior.

–"Big Boy" Maxwell Maltz

Research, research, research!
You need to know your stuff if you want to stay in the game. You don't want to fumble the ball because you couldn't understand

73

the play that was called. Research your industry so you know it inside out and backwards, and don't just stop there. The world is constantly evolving and if you don't keep up with the latest trends, or the FACTS there are studies going on by professionals all the time... read them, and follow the journals, or you're going to be left in the dust.

Here's one I found on the early formation of self esteem issues for girls:

Written By: Kirsten Krahnstoever Davison and Leann Lipps Birch

From the Department of Human Development and Family Studies, Pennsylvania State University, University Park, Pennsylvania.

Objective - This study examined the relationship between weight status and self-concept in a sample of pre-school-aged girls and whether parental concern about child overweight or restriction of access to food are associated with negative self-evaluations among girls.

Method - Participants were 197 5-year-old girls and their parents. Girls' weight status (weight for height percentile) was calculated based on height and weight measurements. Girls' self-concept was assessed using an individually administered questionnaire. Parents' concern about their child's weight status and restriction of their child's access to food were assessed using a self-report questionnaire.

Results - Girls with higher weight status reported lower body esteem and lower perceived cognitive ability than did girls with lower weight status. Independent of girl's weight status, higher paternal concern about child overweight was associated with lower perceived physical ability among girls; higher maternal concern about child overweight was associated with lower perceived physical and cognitive ability among girls. Finally, higher maternal restriction of girls' access to foods was associated with lower perceived physical and cognitive ability among girls with higher weight status but not among girls with lower weight status.

Conclusions - At least as early as age 5 years, lower self-concept is noted among girls with higher weight status. In addition, parents' concern about their child's weight status and restriction of access to food are associated with negative self-evaluations among girls. Public health programs that raise parental awareness of childhood overweight without also providing constructive and blame-free alternatives for addressing child weight problems may be detrimental to children's mental health. Key words: preschool children, weight *status, overweight, self-concept, parent reaction, parent concern, parent restriction.*

Life takes on meaning when you become motivated, set goals and charge after them in an unstoppable manner.
—"Big Boy" Les Brown

A woman has to stay in shape to compete. The reality is, women are still viewed as less competent than men and have to work harder to reach the same goal. Continually research your industry and always keep abreast of trends—this makes you knowledgeable and doesn't allow others to talk over your head.

It also allows quick and smart decisions, and that can distinguish a woman. Men aren't able to do this as well as women because they don't depend on their natural instincts the way women do.

Men may be more interested in holding board meetings or conducting detailed analysis of the situation before making a decision.

However, if someone is well informed, they have the ability to use gut instincts to make a good, if quick, decision.

Even though I didn't have an MBA, I took the reigns of a major corporation and learned the ropes of the rough and tumble food industry through trial and error. I did my homework, kept on top of changes in the business (some would make your head spin!) and built a strong team to promote success.

When I couldn't find the answer I needed in a certain book or on-line, I always asked somebody I admired and knew their stuff, for help—colleagues, experts, my family, even our union. Working together and building allies is definitely the "way to go!"

Never hold back from asking, you will experience an awakening that will ultimately lead you on a path to success and can serve to "level" the playing field.

Not only did this keep more advanced and higher seniority male board members from talking around me, it allowed me to make crucial decisions for the company, including a strategic partnership over an IPO launch, based on research, and supported by gut instinct.

With all the concern around child obesity and lack of exercise with the scary "take over" of sports only on a screen with digitized players on video games, etc. we could learn a lot about this kind of long range dedication from the children's fitness philosophies as we pursue excellence on all levels in our training at www.kidshealth.org

Here are some examples... taken directly from articles on the website, please visit there for more:

Kids exercise all the time without even thinking of it. Just being active, like when you run around outside or play kickball at school, is a kind of exercise. What else counts as exercise? All of these, playing sports, dancing, doing push-ups, and even reaching down to touch your toes.

When you exercise, you're helping build a strong body that will be able to move around and do all the stuff you need it to do. Try to be active every day and your body will thank you later!

Exercise Makes Your Heart Happy

You may know that your heart is a muscle. It works hard, pumping blood every day of your life. You can help this important muscle get stronger by doing aerobic (say: air-o-bik) exercise.

Aerobic means "with air" so therefore aerobic exercise is a kind of activity that requires oxygen. When you breathe, you take in oxygen, and, if you're doing aerobic exercise, you may notice you're breathing faster than normal. Aerobic activity can get your heart pumping, make you sweaty, and quicken your breathing. When your give your heart this kind of workout on a regular basis, your heart will get even better at its main job—delivering oxygen (in the form of oxygen-carrying blood cells) to all parts of your body. So you want to do some aerobic exercise right now? Then try swimming, basketball, ice or roller hockey, jogging (or walking quickly), in-line skating, soccer, cross-country skiing, biking, or rowing. And don't forget that skipping, jumping rope, and playing hopscotch are aerobic activities, too!

Exercise Strengthens Muscles

Another kind of exercise can help make your muscles stronger. Did you ever do a push-up or swing across the monkey bars at the playground? Those are exercises that can build strength. By using your muscles to do powerful things, you can make them stronger. For older teens and adults, this kind of workout can make muscles bigger, too.

Here are some exercises and activities to build strong muscles:
- Push-ups
- Pull-ups

77

- Tug-of-war
- Rowing
- Running
- In-line skating
- Bike riding

Exercise Makes You Flexible

Can you touch your toes easily without yelling ouch? Most kids are pretty flexible, which means that they can bend and stretch their bodies without much trouble. This kind of exercise often feels really good, like when you take a big stretch in the morning after waking up. Being flexible is having "full range of motion," which means you can move your arms and legs freely without feeling tightness or pain. It's easy to find things to do for good flexibility:

- Tumbling and gymnastics
- Yoga
- Dancing, especially ballet
- Martial arts
- Simple stretches, such as touching your toes or side stretches

Exercise Keeps the Balance

Food gives your body fuel in the form of calories, which are a kind of energy. Your body needs a certain amount of calories every day just to function, breathe, walk around, and do all the basic stuff. But if you're active, your body needs an extra measure of calories or energy. If you're not very active, your body won't need as many calories. Whatever your calorie need is, if you eat enough to meet that need, your body weight will stay about the same. If you eat more calories than your body needs, it may be stored as excess fat.

Exercise Makes You Feel Good

It feels good to have a strong, flexible body that can do all the activities you enjoy—like running, jumping, and playing with your friends. It's also fun to be good at something, like scoring a basket, hitting a home run, or perfecting a dive. But you may not know that exercising can actually put you in a better mood.

When you exercise, your brain releases a chemical called endorphins (say: en-dor-funz), which may make you feel happier. It's just another reason why exercise is cool!

Updated and reviewed by: Mary L. Gavin, MD

Date reviewed: June 2004

Originally reviewed by: Heidi Kecskemethy, RD, CSP

COACH'S CORNER:

And, what about "goal setting"...this is an exercise that cannot be ignored!

- How much do you know about your goal? Write down everything you can think of, even if it seems irrelevant or silly at first. For example, if you're trying to lose weight, how much do you know about the different options available to you? Do you know how to shop and cook healthy? Do you know the pros and cons of fad diets seen in the media?
- What things do you not know a lot about that you think would be valuable?
- How can you learn more about the things you've listed?

If there are areas that you feel you're weak in, it's a good to do a "workout" to shape up on those topics. It also never hurts to stay one step ahead of your competition, and there are a few sneaky ways to find out the latest trends and information before they do.

COACH'S CORNER:

Please make a column for each of the items listed below, and leave room to write into the ideas introduced with your own terminology and goals.

1. The Internet

Make the Internet your new best friend. (I still have some friends who have NOT got a clue how to use a computer, and have no intention of learning) YIKES, please do not be one of them... It is very important to stay abreast of the times.

This invaluable tool is an endless source of information about the things you need to know. Even better, it's instant so you have the latest information at your fingertips whenever you need it. Find a search engine you like (I like to "Google" my questions to get the answers) and use it to find the latest news articles about your industry.

2. Conferences

While technology is great, it still pays to invest in some human instruction too. Conferences, seminars or workshops are great places to learn standard and timely things about your industry from experts in that field. The best part is, if you have a question (and you should have lots!) you have someone to answer it.

3. Industry Magazines

While these aren't as current as articles on the Internet, they're still great tools. If you have a subscription, you're promising yourself a monthly dose of relevant information. In every issue, there will always be at least one item that will appeal to you, and it may be something you could follow up. Contact the author or do some research on—you guessed it—the Internet.

4. Online Courses

Perhaps you're not able to get away for a few days to attend that conference that interested you, but don't give up on learning! There are a number of schools that offer online courses for time-strapped people, anywhere from a twelve session training program to a three-year MBA. You choose what fits your schedule.

5. Research Companies

You can subscribe to research companies that, well, research your field for you. For a fee, you can access among other things rising trends, industry statistics and sector analysis.

6. Chat Rooms

Find a chat room related to your industry and log-on. Odds are that the other people in the chat room are either industry experts, or at least work in the field so you can learn tips and new ways of doing business from people around the world. If they aren't experts, they're at least very interested in the industry and you've probably found your target market. Listen, and find out what these people like, hate and want for an edge over your competitors.

NOW:

• Beside each of the items in the first column, list your own ideas of gathering information. For example, beside "Conferences" list some conferences or workshops that are feasible for you to attend.

- Maybe you have other tricks up your sleeve that keep you ahead of the game. List them here. Explain how they help you, and why they're important.

Don't be afraid to ask questions, either! If you read an interesting article, e-mail the author with questions.

When a seminar leader asks if anyone has any questions, don't be afraid, go ahead... put your hand up and ask them one.

The more you seek, the more information you'll find.

CHAPTER FIVE
FOLLOWING THE RULE BOOK

Obstacle to overcome: FEELING UNWORTHY

M — (My)

Feelings of worth can flourish only in an atmosphere where individual differences are appreciated, mistakes are tolerated, communication is open, and rules are flexible—the kind of atmosphere that is found in a nurturing family.

–Virginia Satir

V — (Victory)

Know that although in the eternal scheme of things you are small, you are also unique and irreplaceable, as are all your fellow humans everywhere in the world.

–Margaret Laurence

P — (Plan)

If you have built castles in the air your work need not be lost; that is where they should be. Now put foundations under them.

–Henry David Thoreau

When it comes to the playing field of life, women shouldn't always follow the rulebook. It may be written for and by men who didn't necessarily play "fair," and women and men don't play the game the same way.

Rule book: a collection of rules or prescribed standards on the basis of which decisions are made; "they run things by the book around here"

wordnet.princeton.edu/perl/webwn

This valuable except from:

www.baseballstatistics.com/greats/Century/Moments/Thomson-Branca.htm

The Brooklyn Dodgers were a powerhouse team in the 1940s, led by the talents of Hall of Famers like Pee Wee Reese, Jackie Robinson, Duke Snider and Roy Campanella. Only the Yankees were a better ball club in the late '40s and early '50s. The New York Giants were lovable losers, who hadn't finished better than 5th in the 8-team National League between 1943 and 1950. The bitter rivalry between the Dodgers who played at Ebbett's Field in the Flatbush section of Brooklyn and the Giants, who played at the Polo Grounds in Harlem in the Bronx on Manhattan Island, so divided New Yorkers that they may as well have Confederate Grays and Union Blues.

On August 11, the Giants trailed their cross-town rival Dodgers by 13 1/2 games. Beginning August 12, manager Leo Durocher led his team to 16 consecutive wins, and 37 of their last 44; the Dodgers won 24 of their last 44, a respectable performance, but not enough to prevent the Giants from forging a tie.

New York then played the Dodgers in a best-of-three playoff, with the winner going to the World Series. The

Giants won the first game, 3-1, at Ebbett's Field; the teams took the subway over to the Polo Grounds, where the Dodgers answered with a 10-0 pounding in the Bronx.

In Game 3, the Dodgers' ace Don Newcombe took the mound against Sal Maglie, who had typically pitched well against the Dodgers. The Dodgers scored three runs in the eighth inning to take a 4-1 lead in the decisive third game, and it looked like the Giants were finally out of miracles. Don Newcombe was still pitching well into the ninth, and had allowed only one run in his previous 20 innings of work.

But the Giants' Al Dark got things going with a single; Don Mueller followed with another single, moving Dark to third. Newcombe retired Monte Irvin on a weak popup to Gil Hodges at first. Dodger manager Charley Dressen came out to confer with Newcombe, and decided to leave him in the game.

Then Giants first baseman Whitey Lockman knocked a double, scoring Dark, to make it 4-2. Mueller slid into third, but twisted his ankle and had to be carried off on a stretcher. With the Giants now threatening, Dressen pulled Newcombe and put in Ralph Branca, an effective spot starter who had been 21-12 with a 2.67 ERA in 1947, and who had gone 13-12 with a solid 3.26 ERA in 1951.

Dressen and Branca discussed whether or not to intentionally walk Bobby Thomson, who had 31 homers and 98 RBI that season while batting .292. With first base open and a young, unproven, rookie outfielder named Willie Mays on deck, an intentional walk made sense, but they decided not to put the winning run on base.

Giant's announcer Russ Hodges surveyed the scene, and intoned, "[Pinch runner RHP Clint] Hartung down the line at third, not taking any chances. Lockman without too big a lead at second, but he'll be running like the wind if Thomson hits one."

Branca's first pitch was a called strike, "at the knees" according to Hodges. Thomson dug in, and rocked the second pitch on a low line drive into the left-field stands in the Polo Grounds. Hodges went nuts with the thousands of New York fans in the seats and the millions more listening in on the radio and watching on TV: "The Giants win the pennant! The Giants win the pennant! The Giants win the pennant! The Giants win the pennant! The Giants win the pennant!"

Probably the most famous home run of all time, the Miracle at Coogan's Bluff completed the most dramatic last minute heroics in sports history.

"Now it is done. The art of fiction is dead. Only the impossible, the utterly fantastic, can be plausible again."
                    –New York sportswriter Red Smith

Note: Lost in all the hoopla about the Miracle at Coogan's Bluff is a controversy: were the Giants stealing the signs that the Dodgers' catcher was flashing to Branca?

The following is based largely on research by JOSHUA HARRIS PRAGER, writing for the *Wall Street Journal.*

Baseball can be an ambiguous game. There is no clock, no constancy of the strike zone, and what differentiates a "hit" from an "error" is nothing more than the judgment of the official scorer. Although the spitball has been illegal since 1920, groundskeepers often moisten or dry up the basepaths to benefit the home team—and nowadays, entire ballparks are built and reconfigured to suit the star players on the home teams.

Sign-stealing fits comfortably in its own gray area, like what constitutes sexual relations—players and coaches alike are always trying to see the signals that are used by their opponents to communicate strategy in silence in the 20 or so seconds between every pitch of every baseball game.

Coaches tug their ear lobes, swipe their caps, and adjust their pant legs to hide their intentions, but scouts, coaches and players keep close eyes on their opponents in hopes of glimpsing a pitcher's grip on the ball or deciphering a coach's body language. Runners on second base peer at the catcher's fingers as he signs to the pitcher whether to throw a fastball, curveball or another type of pitch.

16 players and coaches who appeared on the 1951 Giants are dead, but interviews with all 21 surviving players and the one living coach indicate that the 1951 Giants executed an elaborate scheme relying on an electrician and a spyglass. The electrician was one Abraham Chadwick—he was a life-long fan of the Brooklyn Dodgers, but he was employed by the New York Giants at Polo Grounds, not at Brooklyn's Ebbets Field. And the spyglass belonged to one Henry Leonard Schenz, a box of a man with a 48-inch chest and 68-inch frame, who was a utility infielder, played six middling seasons in the Major Leagues.

Some players say, Leo "The Lip" (who is credited with coining the phrase "Nice guys finish last") brought up sign stealing for the first time that year.

"He asked each person if he wanted the sign," says Monte Irvin, the Giants' star left fielder, now 81. "I told him no. He said, "You mean to tell me, if a fat fastball is coming, you don't want to know?" "According to other surviving players, enough of the team did want to know."I'd probably say 50-50," says Al Corwin, a rookie pitcher who joined the Giants that very day. Several players now say that beginning with that meeting, the Giants implemented an elaborate sign-stealing scheme. "Every hitter knew what was coming," says 83-year-old Al Gettel, a pitcher on the 1951 Giants roster into August "Made a big difference."

Jerald Schenz (now 53), the son of Hank Schenz, says that his father occasionally spied signals for his teammates with a telescope from a spot on the scoreboard in Wrigley Field when he played for the Chicago Cubs. "This whole thing began when he was with Chicago," says son Jerald. "They had a spot in the scoreboard at Wrigley. He was out there at times."

One alleged culprit in all of this is Abraham Chadwick, the electrician who had only to turn the park's lights on before games and off afterward. The work lasted five minutes. The rest of the time, Chadwick sat in the stands in his fedora, smoking cigars and watching baseball. According to electricians who knew him, Chadwick installed a bell-and-buzzer system in the clubhouse and connected it to the phones in the bullpen and the dugout. With the press of a button in the clubhouse—once for a fastball, twice for an off-speed pitch—the phones would buzz the sign.

On July 19, a rainout cancelled the Giants' game. On July 20, Giants beat the Reds, 11-5. The Giants took three of four games from the Reds and on July 23 left for Pittsburgh. Brooklyn closed out July with 10 consecutive wins, and an electrician named Seymour Schmelzer replaced Chadwick at the Polo Grounds—Chadwick had stomach cancer, and after surgery, he returned home to the Bronx.

The Giants, meantime, were on their longest road trip of the season, a 17-game swing through Pittsburgh, Cincinnati, Chicago, St. Louis and Brooklyn. They won nine of their first 14 games. But heading into Brooklyn on Aug. 8, they still trailed their rivals by 9 1/2 games. The Dodgers beat the Giants three straight. The gap between the teams ballooned to 12 1/2 games, thus proclaimed Dodgers Manager Charlie Dressen, "The Giants is dead."

Home at last on Aug. 11, the Giants hit rock bottom. They lost to Philadelphia 4-0, and Brooklyn beat Boston 8-1, pushing the Dodgers' lead to 13 1/2 games.

But then everything changed and after losing the series opener the Giants beat Philadelphia three straight, they beat the Dodgers three straight. They again swept three games from the Phillies. They took a pair from Cincinnati and a single game against St. Louis. They beat Chicago four straight. When evening settled on August 27, the Giants had reeled off 16 wins in a row, baseball's longest streak in 16 years. Thirteen of their victories had come at home. They trailed the Dodgers by just five games. By this time, relaying signs from the dugout, where chosen players could shout code words to batters, was deemed too conspicuous. The Giants were mainly relaying signals from the bullpen. The player relaying would sit closest to center field. After hearing the buzzer buzz, he might cross his legs to denote a fastball. He might toss a ball in the air. He might sit still. The method was based, Corwin says, on "what was easiest to see, what was the quickest."

Another change: Schenz was no longer the spy in the clubhouse. He had struggled to decode the opposing catcher's signs. Herman Louis Franks, the Giants third-base coach in 1951, had been a catcher. Like all catchers, he knew signs and how to mask them when runners led off second base. So Franks took Schenz's spot in the clubhouse (and Durocher himself replaced Franks at third base).

Sources: The Educational and Cultural Fund of the Electrical Industry; Barry Halper Baseball Archives; the National Baseball Hall of Fame and Museum Inc.; the Sporting News

Some, like Franks, deny that the Giants ever stole signs. Other players are more forthcoming. Over the first two days of September, the Giants trounced the Dodgers by the combined score of 19 to 3. Mr. Dressen, the Dodgers' skipper, became suspicious. "We took binoculars out on the bench to observe center field," Dodgers coach Cookie Lavagetto told author Harvey Rosenfeld, whose 1992 book *The Great Chase: The Dodgers-Giants Pennant Race of 1951* has two pages devoted to the controversy.

Lavagetto, who died in 1990, continued: "The umpire spotted us. He ran over and grabbed those binoculars away from us. There was nothing we could do. We told the ump that we were just trying to observe center field. Whatever Durocher had out there, he had a good system."

The Dodgers investigated no further. And the Giants continued to win. Winning streaks self-perpetuate. By the time the Giants hit the road in early September, Giants batters had patient, level swings. Giant's pitchers had rested arms. The team won 14 of its final 18 road games, including the last four games of the season. Incredibly, the Giants had overcome a 13 1/2 -game deficit in just 53 days and finished the season tied with the Dodgers: 96 up, 58 down.

Women MVP's…. attention Now! We are in Chapter Five:

Following the "Play by Play" action packed rule book... obstacle to overcome: Feeling Unworthy... Does anyone really win by cheating? You answer that one for yourself.

COACH'S CORNER:

- Write down your dream.
Are you willing to do "ANYTHING" to get it?
What are the rules you have set, or are following, are there any?
- How clearly is your dream defined? How would you describe it to someone else?
- Why would anyone want to sponsor you and your dream?
Why would anyone feel unworthy? Why would you? Is playing fair important to you?
- Give yourself a reasonable time by which you could expect this outcome to occur. You know what you're capable of so be honest with yourself, but also be flexible.
Are you willing to make some concessions, along the way? Some adjustments if needed, even some sacrifices, even, bending of the rules?
- Now brainstorm some "dignified," actions that you would be proud and comfortable taking "right now" to achieve your goal.
If it's to lose weight, then you may want to go for a walk, but start somewhere. If it's to start a business, then write a business plan. You know what needs to be done. If you don't, then begin by writing down what research needs to be done.
- Next, list specific items, actions and short-term goals

that need to be met for you to achieve your goal. Outline the necessary steps you must take in order to get from where you are now to where you want to be. This list is a detailed extension of your previous brainstorming session.

Writing a game plan will help you focus on taking consistent action on your goals and your thoughts so you can begin to access your hidden resources, make progress on what you need to do in order to succeed and anchor that successful behavior in your daily actions.

If you plan to win as I do, the game never ends.
—"Big Boy" Stan Mikita

Let's take a look at the *BIG* picture

When you're in the middle of the game, it's easy to get lost and lose sight of your goal. There's so much excitement between fans critiquing your every move, cheerleaders standing by you to lend support and action taking place right in front of you. With circumstances like these, it's easy to drop the ball.

So how the heck do you stay focused when there are so many distractions around you? Maybe it's not even the distractions that cause you to lose your focus. Perhaps it's you. Maybe you've come up against a tough opponent, one you suspect may even be a cheater! Your opponent isn't backing down, or maybe you threw an interception and doubt has crept into the back of your mind. Whatever the reason, you are questioning yourself and your goal. How do you get back on track, and find the winning play?

Just as important as the challenges you seize is how you tackle those challenges. Develop a framework for your thinking, a framework that calls you to greatness. First, find yourself a Goodyear blimp, grab on and take an aerial view of the field so you can get a good look at the big picture. By focusing on the big picture instead of the many obstacles in the way, it's easier to imagine success.

I LOVE this quote!

Make your life a mission-not an intermission.
–"Big Boy" Arnold H. Glasgow

This sticky sits on my computer, whenever I needed a boost, and reminder about how excited I am about "hitting the field" with Women MVP's everywhere!

Please print it and Post it on your computer or elsewhere, or chose another if it speaks to you… reminders are valuable!

If you think you are beaten, YOU ARE.
If you think you dare not, YOU DON'T.
If you'd like to win but think you can't,
It almost certain that you won't
Life's battles don't always go
To the stronger woman or man,
But sooner or later, those who win
Are those who think they CAN!

COACH'S CORNER:

- Take a good look at your original goal and think about the big picture for a moment. Write down why you set this goal and how you've been working toward it. Why is it important to you?
- What challenges are discouraging you right now? Write them down. Things look a little less scary when

they're on paper!
- What is the most troubling part of each challenge? (Maybe you're having problems getting a bank loan for your small business, but it's the banker you're working with that is causing you the most grief.)
- What are actions you can take right now to overcome these challenges?
- What actions can you take to follow-up your initial action?
- Go back to the first question, and look at the big picture again. Do the challenges you are facing now still seem so big?

Now that you have a clear grasp on the big picture and what it looks like, your next step is to put yourself in that picture.
- Where do you fit in the big picture?
- What is your role?
- List some ways you can keep focused on the big picture, and do not get tied up in any obstacles that try to block you.

Once you visualize success, and remember why you're in this exciting game in the first place, you're on your way to achieving all of your dreams. Your dream is your hopes, longings, and ambitions. Keep dreaming, reach your goals and you will be forever in high spirits!

"Well now fellas" … I do say, as general "rule" women have been known to approach intellectual problems differently than men because their verbal memory is better than that of men. (I'll always remember what you did, said, forgot to do, say, etc, etc.) You've heard it I'm sure.

Sometimes that extended memory stuff is real tragic, and sometimes it is real magic… "Ya you might have Won, I can hear her say… but as I remember it now, *YOU CHEATED, CREEP!*

Yea we girls wouldn't be beyond hiring spies, or peeking now and then, but for heaven's sakes… We like to feel like we played fair… "They deserved that."

We can be more sensitive to the emotions of our teammates on the playing field of life and gain the trust of others easily because of better natural communication and listening skills, humm good thing no women were posted in the spy stands… we'll leave that for the Bond Girls in the movies….

Truth is women can also be better team builders because they establish group cohesion where as men often prefer a hierarchical pecking order.

Let's all play by sometimes setting aside the rules, but not cheating in doing so!

I just bought a great Desk "spiral bound book," by Ed Polish and Darren Wotz … they are fun plays on the traits of "self styled divas and domestic goddesses," quote unquote. These women "have the potential to become "MVP Divas" no less no more!"

Described as tackling womanhood with daring humor and a healthy dose of womanhood with a daring humor and a healthy dose of bitchiness! Definitely not for everyone, but I bought it right away and an extra as a gift, straight away, (the clerk said they can't keep enough in stock, they are flying out the door!

One sticks out in my mind… a Vision in white gloves and adorned in rhinestones… tilted ruby red lips and high arched brows… she advises…

YOU GO GIRL, and take those tacky shoes with you!

Well "back at cha" GUYS I say to the two male authors… described on the package as:

Ed Polish: Owner of Ephemera, Inc, a novelty company specializing in buttons, refrigerator magnets, and other products. Ed never apologizes for his art and he does his own nude scenes. He lives in Ashland Oregon, with his wife Victoria.

Darren Wotz: Does his best to appear productive to the untrained eye. Sarcasm is just one of the services he offers. He lives in Berkley, California, and New York City.

These guys found a market, and I think it is Great to "lighten the load" now and then on the playing field of life… You go fella's and Ladylike Refinement, frivolity, and Merriment on behalf of Women MVP's and their balls everywhere… would tell you to Remember Rule One on the playing field of Life… Ed and Darren…

Always "Shoot to score!"

Women can use their unique perspective to bring new creativity and direction to a project or to a challenge.

COACH'S CORNER:

Find some old vintage photos of female athletes and give them your own "twist"

My" Big Boy" hubby this morning was mentioning to me that he remembers the foo fa rah around the German women in the 50's Olympics that he described as "big hairy brutes," I told him if they heard him they would slap his face—pre steroids these gals were instead given growth hormones!

Have fun with this look up some his/her story!

Barbara Carey took an everyday product and added a female twist.

Standing in the feminine hygiene aisle, she noticed that none of the products had any style. They all looked like medicine, yet Carey didn't feel sick—she just had her period.

From that experience she created Ditties, feminine hygiene products that feature empowering messages on each wrapper.

She created a fun product that doesn't look at a woman's cycle as an ailment. She's kicking taboos to the curb and creating a network of women who are proud to buy, wear and share their Ditties.

You mean…Women can't call in sick, stay on the bench, monthly at least once?

Hustle, hustle girls—That's why you want to be wearing the right gear, dear.

And this fascinating data just in from www.sportsinjuryclinic.net:

Breast Injuries in Female Athletes
What does the breast consist of?

The breasts are composed of mainly fatty tissue with the mammary glands and muscle. The muscle is deep so cannot help much in supporting the breast. Coopers Ligaments help hold the breasts up. They are thin bands interwoven into the breast and are not very strong. If the breasts are not supported properly with a good sports bra then repetitive bouncing from running can stretch the Coopers ligaments permanently

The main injuries affecting breasts are nipple problems (jogger's nipple or friction injury), a direct blow to the breast causing a contusion and repetitive trauma caused by constant movement and bouncing whilst running.

Repetitive trauma injury/ Joggers nipple

Continuous running causes the breasts to move up and down and side to side (Joggers nipple). This not only causes pain resulting from the trauma of excessive movement but will result in permanent stretching of the Coopers ligaments resulting in drooping breasts. It is not just the larger breasted woman suffers breast pain when running but smaller breasted women can often suffer from joggers nipple just as much.

It is also possible that breasts that are not properly supported can lead to tension and strain in the upper back and neck, particularly in the larger breasted woman. The excess weight at the front can mean the back muscles have to work harder to keep the shoulders in the correct position. These muscles will eventually become weak and stretched leading to back and neck pain.

What can the athlete do about it?

• Wear the correct sports bra. This should give support and prevent vertical movement as well as side to side movement.

• 'Breast droop' is irreversible so prevention is better than cure.

• For back pain, try to maintain correct posture with shoulders back. Also a regular sports massage is a great way of reducing the tension in the muscles.

So then where did the sports bra come from?

From …www.Health.com, June 2005

The Sports Bra: An Undercover History
By Amanda Gavlik

Fashion-forward- Comfort-seeking- Fitness-minded-innovators of the brassiere, or "bust supporter," were all these and more. One of the most inventive was Lora Blanche Lyon, who, in 1906, developed and patented the revolutionary whalebone and canvas design. The garment offered 20th century women support that, before, could only be found in constricting corsets that were more painful than pleasurable to wear. Since then, the bra has been re-vamped with luxurious materials and practical designs.

As women became more active, the traditional bra ceased to be functional for high-impact activities. Enter Lisa Lindahl and Hinda Miller, runners who, in 1977, combined two male athletic supporters and a bit of thread to craft the world's first sports bra.

Sexy at 100

In the evolution of the sports bra, it was a long way from whalebone to wow.

With this year's 100th anniversary of the original "bust-supporter," we're celebrating the latest takes on the original contraption made of canvas and whalebone:

(Can you believe that, Whew, from primitive to Prim Donna?)

Now, high-style creations with showy, sexy straps that give you the comfort and support you need you won't want to hide them under a T-shirt anymore!

CHAPTER SIX
THE PLAYING FIELD

Obstacle to overcome: TUNNEL VISION

M — (My)

The most pathetic person in the world is someone who has sight, but no vision.

—Helen Keller

V — (Victory)

Vision is the art of seeing the invisible.

—Jonathan Swift

P — (Plan)

When I dare to be powerful, to use my strength in the service of my vision, then it becomes less and less important whether I am afraid.

—Audre Lorde

Tunnel Vision:

Contraction of the visual field to such an extent that only a small area of central acuity remains, thus giving the affected individual the sensation of looking through a tunnel.

www12.mawebcenters.com/coltslaboratories/gloss.ivnu

Look at the big picture. When you're in the middle of the game, it's easy to get lost and lose sight of your goal. There's so much excitement between fans critiquing your every move, cheerleaders standing by you to lend support and action taking place right in front of you. With circumstances like these, it's easy to drop the ball.

So how the heck do you stay focused when there are so many distractions around you? Maybe it's not even the distractions that cause you to lose your focus. Perhaps it's you. Maybe you've come up against a tough opponent, who isn't backing down, or maybe you threw an interception and doubt has crept into the back of your mind. Whatever the reason, you are questioning yourself and your goal. How do you get back on track, and find the winning play?

Just as important as the challenges you seize is how you tackle those challenges. Develop a framework for your thinking, a framework that calls you to greatness. First, find yourself a Goodyear blimp and take an aerial view of the field so you can get a good look at the big picture. By focusing like these "Wonder Women MVP's" on the big picture instead of the many obstacles in the way, it's easier to imagine and achieve ultimate success.

Top Ten Moments in Women's Sports

From: www.womenssportsfoundation.org/cgi-bin/iowa/events/article.html

This ranking was compiled by ESPN and the Women's Sports Foundation

NUMBER 10... 1943

With America at war and Major League Baseball depleted of players, women step into the batter's box. For 11 years, the All American Girls Professional Baseball League keeps the national pastime alive for fans all over the country. At its peak, in 1948, the league draws nearly a million fans.

NUMBER 9... 1996

Softball and soccer make their Olympic debut at the Games in Atlanta, and the U.S. women dominate! The Americans win gold in softball and soccer, as well as basketball, gymnastics and synchronized swimming. The Games make stars of athletes like Lisa Leslie, Mia Hamm and Lisa Fernandez and give rise to professional softball and soccer leagues in the United States.

NUMBER 8... 1926

American swimming champion Gertrude Ederle becomes the first woman to swim the English Channel—a distance of more than 21 miles. Ederle not only completes the arduous crossing, but she breaks the men's record by almost two hours.

NUMBER 7... 1957

Althea Gibson wins Wimbledon and becomes the first African-American crowned champion at the All-England Club. After her victory in England, Gibson returns stateside, to win the U.S. Championships at Forest Hills. New York honors her with a ticker-tape parade down its Canyon of Heroes.

NUMBER 6... 1932

The United States is in the throes of the great depression, but the country's spirits are lifted by the fearless Amelia Earhart. On the fifth anniversary of Charles Lindberg's historic flight, Earhart becomes the first female pilot to fly solo across the Atlantic.

NUMBER 5... 1999

The Women's World Cup soccer final overtime leads to a shoot-out against China. Overbeck, Fawcett, Lilly, Hamm and Chastain kick for the United States as 90,000 fans in the stadium watch with anticipation. A billion television viewers witness the celebration as the U.S. women take the Cup.

NUMBER 4... 1960

In Rome, Wilma Rudolph becomes the first American woman

to win three gold medals in one Olympic Game. Stricken with polio, Rudolph spent years of her childhood in leg braces before becoming the world's fastest woman. Her courage and perseverance have been an inspiration to generations of young women who followed.

NUMBER 3... 1932

At the Olympic Games in Los Angeles, Mildred "Babe" Didrikson becomes the first woman to take three track and field medals. In her typical fashion, Didrikson wins all the events she competing, but in the high jump, her head-first "western roll" technique is ruled illegal. She set world records in javelin and the 80-meter hurdles, and still holds more medals and records in more sports than any other 20th century athlete.

NUMBER 2... 1972

President Nixon signs Title IX into law, prohibiting federal funding to schools and colleges that exclude women from participating in programs or activities. Title IX enables school girls and collegiate women to compete with the same support the men enjoy. The result has been nothing short of a revolution; since 1971, participation of girls in high school sports has increased from 300,000 to nearly 3 million today.

And the NUMBER ONE Memorable Moment in Women's Sports...

1973... The Astrodome... Billie Jean... Bobby...The Battle of the Sexes... the most watched tennis matches in history.

Houston is suddenly the center of American culture when more than 32,000 fill the Astrodome and another 90 million watch on television as King routs Riggs in three sets. The attendance record still holds today. The match does more to promote the game of tennis than any before it, but this triumph reaches far beyond the tennis court. For many, this is the event that will

define the women's movement of the 1970s and change the
social landscape for women forever.

Women's Sports is also in the "News!"
Now, you can also Find Women's Sports on Television!

COACH'S CORNER:

Pick a Favorite "Sports HERO moment" and do a comparative with the Herion and yourself... learn from their example, you may be surprised how much you already have in common!

Then work to apply the special mentoring principles of their positive examples on your own "playing field!"

- Take a good look at your original goal and think about the big picture for a moment. Write down why you set this goal and how you've been working toward it. Why is it important to you?
- What challenges are discouraging you right now? Write them down. Things look a little less scary when they're on paper!
- What is the most troubling part of each challenge? (Maybe you're having problems getting a bank loan for your small business, but it's the banker you're working with that is causing you the most grief.)
- What are actions you can take right now to overcome these challenges?
- What actions can you take to follow-up your initial action?
- Go back to the first question, and look at the big picture again. Do the challenges you are facing now still seem so big?

Now that you have a clear grasp on the big picture and what it looks like, your next step is to put yourself in that picture.

- **Where do you fit in the big picture?**
- **What is your role?**
- **List some ways you can keep focused on the big picture, and to not get tied up in any obstacles that try to block you.**

Once you visualize success, and remember why you're in this game in the first place, you're on your way to achieving all of your dreams. Your dream is your hopes, longings, and ambitions. Keep dreaming, reach your goals and you will be forever in high spirits!

Like the gridiron, there are continual obstacles in life—things that get in your way and attempt to prevent you from reaching the goal line. The biggest challenge facing women in business is social norms that question women's ability and responsibility. This can be a huge barrier to success, either as an entrepreneur and business owner or to a corporate career woman.

Your goal is your dream. Work to achieve it!

See it, Believe it, and Feel It!

In other words Claim it NOW

Just as important as the challenges women seize is how they tackle those challenges. Women need to develop a framework for their thinking, a framework that calls them to greatness. First, recognize the "big picture." Then, figure out how to be a part of that picture. By focusing on the "big picture" instead of the many obstacles in the way, it's easier to imagine success. Once you visualize success, your chances of achieving it improve.

An Australian friend of mine named Margaret has come up

against many personal and professional obstacles in her rise to the top but continued to keep the "big picture" in mind.

She suffered from a lack of education, abuse, debt and a tragic car accident that left her infant child dead and Margaret in the hospital for nine months.

She was "pegged" a "dunce" ... and told very negative things about her potential and her place in this world.

Take it with a "grin" of salt.

–"Big Boy" Yogi Berra

A dunce cap, (never a good idea for any team to adapt) also variously known as a dunce hat, dunce's cap, or dunce's hat, is a pointy hat. In popular culture, it is typically made of paper and often marked with a D, and given to schoolchildren to wear as punishment for being stupid or lazy.

(sounds pretty idiotic to me already, designed by some control freak no doubt)

While this is now a rare practice, it is frequently depicted in popular culture such as children's cartoons. Such headwear is most prevalent in Western culture but achieved certain prevalence in modern China in connection with various elements of the communist movement.

Origins

The word "dunce" was originally a reference to John Duns Scotus, a 13th century scholastic theologian, whose books on theology, philosophy, and logic were University textbooks. His followers, termed "Dunsmen" or "Dunses", were later challenged about their hodgepodge system of hair-splitting and needless distinctions. Their obstinacy over an increasing array of challenges posed first by humanists and then by reformers, led to the term "dunses" to denote fools in general.

According to the *Oxford English Dictionary* (2nd edition), "dunce cap" didn't enter the language until after the term "dunce" was so transformed. John Ford's 1624 play The Sun's Darling is the first recorded mention of the related term "dunce table," a table provided for duller or poorer students; "dunce cap" appears first in the 1840 novel *The Old Curiosity Shop* by Charles Dickens.

The Straight Dope notes that Duns Scotus accepted the wearing of conical hats to increase learning, in the belief that it would funnel knowledge to its wearer (and perhaps in emulation of wizards).

She gathered up her strength, took off the invisible cap that was placed on her pretty head, and replaced it with what she deserved to wear instead, the winning team's jersey and a helmet for protection and showed her own true colors as she took to the field!

Future Woman MVP Margaret not only survived, she was able to move ahead.

The best way to get beyond being "labeled" is to understand the playing field. To calmly come to understand origins... and speak intelligently from an understanding and knowing of where, how and why these nutty ideas come into existence?

You Know, The Clint Eastwood in you... "Go ahead make my Day!" attitude... gun laws aside... "Tough it out and toughen up a bit, girl!"

Margaret entered the male world of real estate and despite her humble beginnings she built a real estate company that now has sales in excess of $1 billion. She is considered a property guru of Australia's Gold Coast and has significant interests in Southeast Asia, the United Kingdom, South America and North America. She Rocks!

I have been privileged and honored to have been included in the fine works of some of the publications of Self Growth efforts.

I found this piece from another "Coach" who has shared openly and honestly for all of us who have felt at one time or another, like Margaret, or any "Competitive playing field" we may have entered, or feel we fell victim to...for that matter ... We can feel that we are being "beaten down."

This wisdom shared from an article posted on www.selfgrowth.com

Beaten Down ... Being the victim of one-upmanship!
—"Big Boy" Edward B. Toupin

Edward B. Toupin is an author, life-strategy coach, counselor, and technical writer living in Las Vegas, NV. Among other things, he authors books and articles on topics ranging from career success through life organization and fulfillment. For more information, e-mail Edward at etoupin@toupin.com or visit his sites at http://www.make-life-great.com or http://www.make-life-great.com.

It's a funny world in which we live. Some people want badly to succeed. Others want badly to see others fail. Although this might sound a bit pessimistic, it is truly another example of balance in our world.

For every success, we must have a failure. For every positively motivated individual, we must have one who is negatively motivated. It is a fact of life, but many people are blind-sided because it is hard to believe that people would purposefully work to bring others to defeat.

One-Upmanship

There are many definitions of one-upmanship. Some see it as the situation we all encountered in elementary school: "my daddy's bigger than your daddy". But, as we grow, the competition grows and the stakes become greater. When we can no longer compare "dads to dads" and begin to rely on our own traits and abilities, some people tend to fall behind.

These people begin to realize that they can no longer compete and they claw and grab to pull others down so that they can feel better about themselves.

I think my grandfather provided the perfect example. Sometimes humanity is like a pot of boiling crabs. As the water heats up, the crabs on the bottom grab at the ones immediately above to crawl out. In the process, the higher crabs are pushed to the bottom, which then begin to claw their way out. This vicious cycle continues until all crabs are boiled! Indeed, this is not a valiant comparison of the human condition, but it is truer than you might think and something that you may encounter every day without knowing it.

Projected Control

It is sometimes easier for us to control others when indeed we cannot control ourselves. To control ourselves, we have to know ourselves. However, instead of taking the time to look at our attributes and deficiencies, we project them on to others and turn these other people into "puppets" of ourselves. By controlling others on whom we've projected ourselves, we are, in essence, feeling in control of ourselves.

In this way, it is easier to keep others down because we are afraid to face our own inadequacies. But, since the life objective of such a person would be to keep others down, they have no time or room for other activities that could potentially enhance their lives. Yes, some people will do what they can to "bamboozle" you to get what they can ... it's not paranoia ... it is fact. But, if you can accept that fact and learn that you don't have to conform, then you're all the better for it. But, the way they treat me ...

Mr. Toupin is a "Big Boy!" with lots of wisdom to share, thanks dear friend!

You wouldn't have won if we'd beaten you.
—"Big Boy" Yogi Berra

COACH'S CORNER:

If you are the victim of one-upmanship, try to analyze where the other party is coming from before passing judgment on yourself. In many cases, you will find that the other party is only lashing out because of something that they're lacking in themselves.

I need their acceptance...

Occasionally, we accept the "beatings" that are given to us by others simply to make it through the day. Realize that negative energy breeds more negative energy; however, positive energy takes effort and concentration because it oscillates at such a higher frequency. Therefore, it is easy to fall prey to one-upmanship and negative energies because it does not take as much effort.

HALF the lies they tell about me aren't true.
—"Big Boy" Yogi Berra

Learn to look within yourself for appreciation and acceptance and give yourself permission to seek a better and more fulfilling life every day. It is not in how others treat you that can make a difference in your life, but it is in how you treat yourself.

These Men are some the "Big Boys" out there on the "Playing Field of Life!" They share wisdom we all need to hear, and they do so from the perspective of intelligent thought and dreams for our freedom from Obstacles that get distorted and can hold us back.. Let's meet another "Big Boy," who journeyed through Hell, and came up for air to share in a positive way, without being, "taken down."

Darrell Scott Testimony on Columbine
(Verified at Truth or Fiction)

Here is an excerpt from the "Playing field of Life" where it can really be a rough and tumble tough game; we are all sometimes called to still stay in the game, and the playoffs! The words of this Life coach ring loud and true for many.

DARRELL SCOTT TESTIMONY

Darrell Scott, the father of Rachel Scott, a victim of the Columbine High

School shootings in Littleton, Colorado, was invited to address the House Judiciary Committee's subcommittee What he said to our national leaders during this special session of Congress was painfully truthful. They were not prepared for what he was to say, nor was it received well. It needs to be heard by every parent, every teacher, every politician, every sociologist every psychologist, and every so-called expert! These courageous words spoken by Darrell Scott are powerful, penetrating, and deeply personal.

There is no doubt that God sent this man as a voice crying in the wilderness. The following is a portion of the transcript:

"Since the dawn of creation there has been both good & evil in the hearts of men and women, we all contain the seeds of kindness or the seeds of violence. The death of my wonderful daughter, Rachel Joy Scott, and the deaths of that heroic teacher, and the other eleven children who died must not be in vain. Their blood cries out for answers.

The first recorded act of violence was when Cain slew his brother Abel out in the field. The villain was not the club he used. Neither was it the NCA, the National Club Association. The true killer was Cain, and the reason for the murder could only be found in Cain's heart. In the days that followed the Columbine tragedy, I was amazed at how quickly fingers began to be pointed at groups such as the NRA. I am not a member of the NRA. I am not a hunter. I do not even own a gun. I am not here to represent or defend the NRA—because I don't believe that they are responsible for my daughter's death. Therefore I do not believe that they need to be defended. If I believed they had anything to do with Rachel's murder I would be their strongest opponent.

I am here today to declare that Columbine was not just a tragedy-it was a spiritual event that should be forcing us to look at where the real blame lies! Much of the blame lies here in this room. Much of the blame lies behind the pointing fingers of the accusers themselves. I wrote a poem just four nights ago that expresses my feelings best. This was written way before I knew I would be speaking here today:

Your laws ignore our deepest needs,
Your words are empty air.
You've stripped away our heritage,
You've outlawed simple prayer.

Now gunshots fill our classrooms,
And precious children die.
You seek for answers everywhere,
And ask the question "Why?"
You regulate restrictive laws,
Through legislative creed
And yet you fail to understand,
That God is what we need!

Men and women are three-part beings. We all consist of body, soul, and spirit. When we refuse to acknowledge a third part of our make-up, we create a void that allows evil, prejudice, and hatred to rush in and wreak havoc.

Spiritual presences were present within our educational systems for most of our nation's history. Many of our major colleges began as theological seminaries. This is a historical fact. What has happened to us as a nation?

We have refused to honor God, and in so doing, we open the doors to hatred and violence. And when something as terrible as Columbine's tragedy occurs, the real villain lies within our own hearts

As my son Craig lie under that table in the school library and saw his two friends murdered before his very eyes-He did not hesitate to pray in school. I defy any law or politician to deny him that right! I challenge every young person in America, and around the world, to realize that on April 20, 1999, at Columbine High School prayer was brought back to our schools. Do not let the many prayers offered by those students be in vain.

Dare to move into the new millennium with a sacred disregard for legislation that violates your God-given right to communicate with Him.

Dare to examine your own heart before casting the first stone! My daughter's death will not be in vain! The young people of this country will not allow that to happen!

COACH'S CORNER:

Even if it hurts, at first, dress up and show up on the playing field anyway... be willing to "learn the plays" that are used to out maneuver...Listen to others whether you agree or not. Listening, being compassionate and respecting is the first step of any Win/Win exchange.

Try with all your heart, give it all you've got, to look inside and see the facts as you know them to be true of circumstances that have hit you down to the ground, and even "trampled" you, left you paralyzed, or given you sports injuries that just cannot seem to be massaged away.

Take a lesson from the "aerial View" taken by the coaches here in Chapter Six, and "run the ball, with a view!"

Get "touched up as you get that "touch down!"

Weigh it all, Way down, down deep. Let yourself "turn a few things over." Coach others along the way, and teach by your example.

That stuff was "last season stuff," get with the program... we are entering a new season with the dawning of a new scoreboard, with new games to be tabulated."

There really is a light at the end of that "tunnel Vision!"

Stop being myopic ... Look into the tunnel, overcome that obstacle, Go into it and you will win the day for yourself, your team, and everyone in the stands!

No One or no thing can stop you now; YOU Go Girl, YOU MVP, YOU!

This exerpt from an article titled: Male execs like female coaches (Get's my vote!)

By Del Jones, *USA TODAY*

Men hold 94% of the highest corporate jobs, but they usually turn to women when they want the advice of an executive coach.

- InterCoach, an executive coaching company, kept one man on its eight-person staff — for awhile. "Nobody asked for him," so he resigned, says InterCoach President Laura Berman Fortgang, author of *Take you to the Top: The Secrets of America's #1 Career Coach.*

- George Habel, vice president for Capitol Broadcasting, says the company offers coaching to its highest executives. The executives can choose the gender of the coach, but only one has selected a man. Many of Capitol's executives run minor league baseball teams, and all rate at least an 8 on "a macho scale to 10," Habel says. "In their worklife, they're competing primarily with men. In the end, they're just more comfortable talking to a woman."

- When Cambria Consulting needed a partner to develop its strategic executive coaching practice, it chose Ellen Kumata, whose clients have included Deloitte & Touche, Fortis, Gap, J.P. Morgan Chase, Merrill Lynch, MetLife and Wachovia. "Generally speaking, that profile tends to fit women better," Vilas says. "CEOs are hard-charging, Jack Welch-type people. They recognize, in order to be balanced, they need a softer side."

"The fantasy is that women will listen better," says Susan Bloch, who heads the 120-person executive coaching practice at the Hay Group.

"When a man is asked to coach another, they have a tendency to compete. Man to man, they have to show each other how great they are."

Women fill 6.2% of the corporate "line" positions, those with profit-and-loss responsibility, according to Catalyst, a non-profit organization to advance women in business.

The first convention, in 1996, drew 250. Today, there are about 15,000 coaches, and that number is expanding by about 200 a month, according to the International Coach Federation.

Unlike consultants, coaches are not experts in the business and are not hired to give advice about the day-to-day operations of the company. They are trained listeners who help with goals and personal problems.

Coaches say they spend a lot of time on the personal lives of striving male executives, which are commonly a wreck. Executives often complain of bad marriages and the inability to make it to their children's ballgames.

COACH'S CORNER:

Team up with another woman MVP or a "Big Boy" ... and play the roles.

One coach one player... then the other coach and the other are the player...

Video tape your interchange... then do an "instant Replay!"

Watch the moves, reactions and results, "draft an action Plan!"

Use examples you have learned about through your learning with the Wonder Women and Big Boys here in Woman MVP, please do make reference notes and pull coach's corner guidance from past exercises to support your decisions for your next moves and/or justification for past moves, or lack of them!

CHAPTER SEVEN
RUNNING THE BALL

Obstacle to Overcome:
UGLY DUCKLING SYNDROME

M — (My)

To will is to select a goal, determine a course of action that will bring one to that goal, and then hold to that action till the goal is reached. The key is action.

–Michael Hanson

V — (Victory)

Nothing is given to man on earth—struggle is built into the nature of life, and conflict is possible—the hero is the man who lets no obstacle prevent him from pursuing the values he has chosen.

–Andrew Bernstein

P — (Plan)

An excuse becomes an obstacle in your journey to success when it is made in place of your best effort or when it is used as the object of the blame.

–Bo Bennett

Women need to run the ball differently than men because they face different obstacles. In business, while men are expected to be the breadwinners and to advance their careers at any cost, women are expected to be wives and mothers first, career women last, if at all.

Ugly duckling (*n*) (an ugly or unpromising child who grows into a beautiful or worthy person)

wordnet.princeton.edu

Women, not men, are expected to handle issues like childcare, balancing work with home and maintaining healthy personal relationships with their partner and friends. A woman with commitments at home is in for a rough ride. The expectation is for women to be readily available at home and also at work.

The only way to succeed in Life and business is to recognize that there are several important areas to maneuver.

Find a balance that works by devoting a specific amount of time each day to these different areas, including some personal time to exercise (mind and body and spirit) relax and reenergize.

You've also got to accept that sometimes life is just out of balance, and that's the way it is—at least temporarily. Attitude is everything, keep your attitude at a high level…balance will follow.

One woman who has found the right balance as she runs for "touchdown after touchdown" is American author, Dr. Susan Jeffers. She married young and quickly had two children but realized she was meant to do something more than raise a family. Despite being told that a woman's place was in the home, Susan went back to school when her children were young and attained her BA, Masters and Doctorate in Psychology. Following her graduation, this working mother took on the project of writing her first book, Feel the

Fear and Do It Anyway! The manuscript was rejected many, many times but Susan had dedicated time in her life to this project and she saw it through. An editor eventually agreed to publish the book and since then, she has many... many more books and audio series to her credit.

When I was 40, my doctor advised me that a man in his 40s shouldn't play tennis. I heeded his advice carefully and could hardly wait until I reached 50 to start again.
—"Big Boy" Hugo Black

Find balance—Everybody's definition of balance is different. For me, it's finding a way to give time to my family, my career and myself. And I'll tell you, it sure has its complexities. It's very easy to neglect one thing to favor another, especially if you're feeling pressure to give more time than you have. Maybe your boss is demanding a lot of overtime hours, or your child wants you to be at all of his or her ball games. Or maybe you've managed to fill your work and family obligations but at the end of the day, you haven't even taken five minutes for yourself.

It's important that you find a balance that works for you, and fulfills all of your needs. There's no point spending three extra hours at the office if you're going to be guilt-ridden over skipping your child's school play.

It is time for us to stand and cheer for the doer, the achiever, the one who recognizes the challenge and does something about it.
—"Big Boy" Vince Lombardi

You are well on your way to becoming a "Woman MVP," You Go Girl!

Here is a "brief winner blip... on another Woman MVP, from her website...www.susanjeffers.com

Who is Susan Jeffers?
The "Official" Bio

Susan Jeffers, Ph.D. has helped millions of people throughout the world overcome their fears, heal their relationships, and move forward in life with confidence and love.

She is the author of many internationally renowned books including Feel the Fear and Do It Anyway, Feel the Fear . . . and Beyond, Feel the Fear Power Planner, End the Struggle and Dance With Life, Dare to Connect, Opening Our Hearts to Men, Losing a Love...Finding a Life, Thoughts Of Power and Love, The Little Book of Confidence, Embracing Uncertainty, Life is Huge! Plus her "Fear-less Series" of affirmation books and tapes (Inner Talk for Peace of Mind, Inner Talk for a Confident Day, and Inner Talk For a Love That Works). Her latest book is The Feel the Fear Guide to Lasting Love, which was published in the UK in May 2005 and in the US and Canada by her own publishing company, Jeffers Press, in October 2005.

As well as being a best-selling author, Susan is a sought-after public speaker and has been a guest on many radio and television shows internationally. She lives with her husband, Mark Shelmerdine, in Los Angeles.

What makes the work of Susan Jeffers stand out? A look at the masses of thank-you letters she receives reveals that her fans—young and old, and from a whole array of life situations—love her humanness, her humor, her willingness to reveal so much of herself, the universality of her message, and the easy-to-understand style of her writing...a winning combination, indeed. They report, "It's as though she is speaking directly to me." The connection is truly felt. And connection is what Susan Jeffers is all about.

"Susan Jeffers is attractive, articulate, artfully commanding..."

—Los Angeles Times

The "Unofficial" Bio

I think of myself as someone who seems to be constantly reinventing herself. I started out as a small town girl and became a big city woman. I love big cities! In my early life, I lived by the then-rules, which means I got married early and had two children. It didn't take long for me to realize that the rules really weren't written for me. I was meant to be doing something in addition to raising a family.

I went back to school when my children were young, much to the shock of my mother and others who felt a woman's place was definitely in the home. I felt this was true only for women who wanted to be there...and not true for those who didn't! So I persevered and attained my BA, Masters Degree, and Doctorate in Psychology.

Fate stepped in upon graduation and offered me the opportunity to become Executive Director of The Floating Hospital, New York's Ship of Health. At the same time, my husband and I decided to end our marriage of 16 years. Thankfully, we are good friends today. I call his present wife, my wife-in-law.

My ten years at The Floating Hospital and my life as a single woman were intensely gratifying and exciting. What an adventure! I certainly learned a lot about feeling the fear and doing it anyway! It was also during those ten years that I began my journey to self-discovery that was to make me a happier and more loving person, and led me into my present career of writing self-help books.

Just when I felt it was time to leave THE FLOATING HOSPITAL and begin my new writing career, I fell in love with the wonderful Englishman to whom I am now married, Mark Shelmerdine, and gained two step-children.

Mark owned London Films and produced such television series as I Claudius, Poldark, The Scarlet Pimpernel and many others. Most importantly, he loved, kind, giving, and cute...and he dearly loved this woman...even though she only had one breast as a result of a mastectomy. (Truly, women out there, those breasts aren't really that important!) Mark calls me his "titless wonder", which makes me feel very special and tells me I look like a sexy pirate. We are now married 20 years and it just gets better... and better...and better...and better.

My new career took a while to take hold. It took many, many rejections before my first book, FEEL THE FEAR AND DO IT ANYWAY, was finally accepted by a publisher. The worst rejection letter I ever got was that "Lady Di could be bicycling nude down the street giving this book away and nobody would read it."

You would have thought the book would end up in the trash bin at this point. But undaunted, I moved forward and with the help of my genius agent, Dominick Abel, my writing career was finally launched. In 1986, a wonderful editor at Harcourt Brace Jovanovich named Martha Lawrence said YES! (She is now a talented writer of mystery books.) The valuable lesson I learned was never give up if you believe in something!

Well, that's it in a nutshell. What is the next step of the Journey? Only time will tell. I'll keep you posted.

COACH'S CORNER:
Write your own Unoofical and Official biograpghy to date:
(Remember to "keep it real, on both fronts!")

There is an old song called "Billy Boy" that talks about a man going to find himself a wife. One verse goes:

Can she make a cherry pie?
Billy Boy, Billy Boy?
Can she make a cherry pie?
Charming Billy?
She can make a cherry pie,
Quick as a cat can wink an eye,
She's a young thing
And cannot leave her mother

I think about Ann Taintor's vintage products, and I can visualize a pretty little thing in an apron making this cherry pie while good old Billy Boy sits at the table and imagines her working in his own kitchen.

But if Ann was able to put her twist on it, I bet the picture would look a lot different. The lovely "young thing" would be making a cherry pie—but it sure wouldn't be for Billy Boy. It would be to help her find balance in her life, or perhaps a graph on her latest corporate endeavor, she would have on her "thinking cap!" and the colors of her team!

I imagine my time and budget much like a cherry (or blueberry, or apple—whichever you prefer!) pie. I get to choose what size piece I cut for every body.

COACH'S CORNER:

You don't have to cut your pie into six equal pieces, but instead, you can cut the pieces to meet the needs of what's important to you. This also means you don't have to divide the pie according to what people expect of you. There's always someone who demands the biggest piece, but accommodating everybody but you is just the pits!

CHAPTER EIGHT
THE REFS CALL IT

Obstacle to overcome:
COULDA WOULDA SHOULDA

M — (My)

The first thing is to love your sport. Never do it to please someone else. It has to be yours.

–Peggy Fleming

V — (Victory)

If a problem is undermining you, the smallest performance becomes an insuperable obstacle. You dread it. Then, miraculously, you clear the hurdle.

–Placido Domingo

P — (Plan)

Nothing stops the man who desires to achieve. Every obstacle is simply a course to develop his achievement muscle. It's a strengthening of his powers of accomplishment.

–Thomas Carlyle

There are always going to be referees in life, people who are ready to call the game how they see it. These people can hold stereotypes of women in general and in business, or have preconceived ideas of the role women play in society (and that role often isn't in the business world). Regardless, they penalize businesswomen with harsh judgments.

Assess the criticism—is any of it valuable, truthful or constructive? Or is it merely a biased attack? Always remember to take what's valid and leave what's not. Constructive criticism enables leaders to see the holes in their game plan and adjust it to move on to success.

"Wonder Woman" CELINE DION LYRICS

"Coulda Woulda Shoulda"
Did you ever fall in love
At the right time or place
Does it always have to move
At its own kinda pace

When you're driving on cruise control
Coming up a bumpy ride
And your heart is back in shape
Then it hits you with no chance to hide

But don't you miss out on the way
Don't find a reason to say

Coulda Woulda Shoulda
But I didn't do that
(You gotta) Give it a shot
Better believe
And don't say you...

Coulda Woulda Shoulda
(But I didn't do that)
Just throw in everything you've got
Coz in love there's no holding back

Hear that, "No holding back!" Women MVP's in training...
remember that when you're on the playing field of life and it's all or
nothing.

The "Dean of NFL Referees"

"Big Boy" JIM TUNNEY had an exemplary career as an NFL refer-
ee (1960–1991). The first official to be named to the "All-Madden
Team," Jim also won top honors from the National Association of
Sports Officials, the Gold Whistle Award (1992), and is in the
National Football League Hall of Fame.

In his 31 years as an NFL official, Tunney received a record 29
postseason assignments, including ten Championships and three
Super Bowls. Highlights of his career include these classic games:

SUPER BOWL VI

SUPER BOWL XI

SUPER BOWL XII

Still active in NFL affairs and many sports issues, Tunney regu-
larly suggests rule changes and ways to improve the game. He continues to serve his community in many ways. He is the Chair of the
Monterey Peninsula Community College and serves on several
boards of directors: namely the Central Coast Chapter of the
National Football Foundation and on the Bay Area Sports Hall of
Fame.

A celebrated and respected speaker, Tunney's credentials place
him in the top 1% of professional speakers working today. A past-

president of the National Speakers Association, he is a mentor to many members. Known for his ability to educate, motivate and entertain, Tunney works with national and international corporations and organizations.

Have you ever watched a sports game when the referee or umpire made an obviously bad call? No amount of booing from the fans, or hissy-fits from the coach changed the ref's mind. Maybe this call didn't have a big impact on the game's result, or maybe it altered the results for the worse.

On Cheating

(As you might imagine, Jim reads the sports pages pretty thoroughly. Sometimes he writes in response. The following opinion appeared in USA Today...)

In NFL, cheating is for losers, not for winners

Former Atlanta Falcon Tim Green is a talented, forthright sports commentator. He riled me, though, saying "you cheat to win and because you can" in the National Football League "Cheating to win is rule of thumb for teams' survival," Commentary, Sports, Nov. 9).

Did Bart Starr, Johnny Unitas, Roger Staubach, Merlin Olsen cheat to win? Did Vince Lombardi, Tom Landry, Chuck Noll, Bill Walsh or Don Shula cheat to win? How many Hall-of-Famers should I list?

Green says that when Rod Woodson, San Francisco cornerback, interfered with Dallas wide receiver Michael Irvin near the goal line Nov 2 to beat the Cowboys, he was "cheating to win."

Green is wrong on motive and rules interpretation. There was no defensive pass interference. The flag initially thrown by the back judge was picked up because *The Official Rules say,* "Inadvertent tripping is not a foul." Unless the contact is a material restriction or impedes the opponent, all contact is incidental. The NFL officiating department upheld the no-call through unanimous review by the eight supervisors. There was no interference.

Indeed, Woodson and every self-respecting corner would be embarrassed for Green or anyone to suggest that they couldn't defend Irvin or any receiver without "cheatin'."

Green quotes his old coach at Atlanta, Jerry Glanville, as insisting, "if you ain't cheatin', you ain't trying.'" If this is true, I better understand the Falcons' win-loss record during Glanville's tenure.

Further, I've known the current coach at Atlanta, Dan Reeves, for more than 25 years, from his days as a player for Dallas and coach for Dallas, Denver, New York and now Atlanta. Trust me on this: Reeves doesn't buy into Green's cheatin' stuff. He knows football, how to coach skills and motivate toward excellence. These get you into the end zone a whole lot faster than yielding penalty yards to the opponent.

Tim Green missed this tackle. Skills, commitment, talent, training and team work are game-winning skills in the NFL and at every level of athletics. Cheating does not fool officials, fans or coaches. It is not a tool for success—Ever.

  –"Big Boy" Jim Tunney, NFL referee 1960–91

Guess what, ladies?

There are referees in life too and you could very well be the target of a really bad call, or a GREAT call that you simply resent. We have all had a situation in our lives where we have allowed others to underestimate us, or where we were misjudged, or where we stubbornly simply didn't want to hear about it! Someone is always there with ready criticism, in the "Peanut gallery of life."

Do you believe what they say at the risk of giving up your dream, or do you tune them out completely, even if they, made a "fair and square" observation and simply "call it" like it is.

My motto was always to keep swinging. Whether I was in a slump or feeling badly or having trouble off the field, the only thing to do was keep swinging.

–"Big Boy" Hank Aaron

COACH'S CORNER:

- Describe a situation where someone harshly criticized you or your actions, and you stopped what you were doing because of it. Why did you take their criticism seriously? How did it make you feel?
- Describe a situation where someone harshly criticized you or your actions, and you ignored them and continued on. What did you do to dispel their judgment? How did it make you feel?

While I'm an advocate of tuning out naysayers, I always caution people about numbing yourself to them. Be careful—there is a difference. It's never a bad thing to take in criticism and evaluate it. Is any of it valuable, truthful or constructive? Or is it simply a biased attack?

- Look at your answers for the first two questions of this session. Was the criticism in your first example constructive or crap? Did the criticism you ignored in the second situation have any value in it?

- **How would the first situation have been different if you had ignored the criticism? How would the second situation have been different if you had listened to it? Do you regret either decision?**

Even bad criticism can serve a purpose, if it's constructive. While you may be miffed or feel it may not be valuable for your actions at the time, it can alert you to a hole in your overall game plan. An offhand comment about the sparkly, new tennis bracelet you're sporting may seem like petty jealously, but it does throw your spending habits into question. If your end goal is to save and invest properly so you can retire at 40, is a $3,000 diamond bracelet helping your cause, if yes and you can justify how and why... then you call the plays fair, and referee Your own game too now and then.

Always remember to take what's valuable and leave behind what's not.

NOTE: Every year, I proudly give the Fred Mitchell-Memorial Scholarship, it is awarded to a young woman with a troubled past. If anyone has faced criticism, it is the recipients of this award, which goes toward education costs to help them find a future.

One of the recipients was barely living in a tiny room at the YMCA while under the financial struggle of post-secondary education. When LuAn met her for lunch, she seemed very nervous about removing her beat up leather coat to reveal the brazen tattoos that covered her exposed skin. While others in her life criticized her poor lifestyle, she seemed more concerned with what LuAn thought about her body art. After winning the award, she maintained a 77% average and went on to become a social worker. These women may not be CEOs but they are Women MVP's on their own journeys and successes in their own right and in their own lives.

Testimonials from some of these MVP's can be read and experienced at www.LuAnMitchell.com

They have served their time, and have now taken to the field to "Tackle the NOW!" No "woulda coulda shoulda" bench warmers, these gals have spunk!

Tackle The Thing
Somebody said that it couldn't be done,
But he with a chuckle replied
That "maybe it couldn't," but he would be one
Who wouldn't say so till he tried.
So he buckled right in with a trace of a grin
on his face. If he worried he hid it.
He started to sing as he tackled the thing
that couldn't be done, and did it.
Somebody scoffed: Oh, you'll never do that;
At least no one has ever done it";
But he took off his coat and he took off his hat,
And the first thing we knew he'd begun it.
With a lift of his chin and a bit of a grin,
Without any doubting or quid it.
He started to sing as he tackled the thing
that couldn't be done, and did it.
There are thousands to tell you it cannot be done,
There are thousands to prophesy failure;
There are thousands to point out to you, one by one,
The dangers that wait to assail you.
But just buckle in with a bit of a grin,
Just take off your coat and go to it;
Just start to sing as you tackle the thing
That "cannot be done," and you'll do it.

Edgar A. Guest

"Big Boy" Edgar Guest

From Wikipedia, the free encyclopedia

Edgar Albert Guest (August 20, 1881 – August 5, 1959) was a prolific United States poet popular in the first half of the 20th century.

Born in Birmingham, Warwickshire, England, his family moved to the U.S. in 1891. In 1902, he became a naturalized citizen. Beginning at the *Detroit Free Press* as a reporter, he later began writing daily poems which were syndicated to newspapers throughout the U.S. For forty years, his poems were generally simple and positive and written about everyday life. He was made Poet Laureate of Michigan. Edgar Guest died in Detroit, Michigan. His work still occasionally appears in periodicals such as *Reader's Digest*.

Do Winning Coaches foster more winners? Who can coach others... as Woman MVPs? I think Mr. Guest gets a "thumbs up!"
Well maybe....
His great-niece Judith Guest is a successful novelist who wrote *Ordinary People*.

"Wonder Woman" Judith Guest

From Wikipedia, the free encyclopedia

Judith Guest (born March 29, 1936), in Detroit, Michigan) is an American novelist and screenwriter.

So then, who is your coach? Do you have one or many? Cheerleaders can help us too! Rah Rah.... Sis Boom Bah!

133

On Making Excuses

(From a *Referee* Magazine writing—it touches upon some of the thoughts which led to Jim Tunnel wanting to compile Chicken Soup for the Sports Fan's Soul.)

I have a difficult time giving sympathy to people who make excuses for their bad behavior by denying they made the decisions that took them there.

You've heard the gamut: "...It was the booze talking ... I didn't think anyone would find out..." The number of copouts is endless. Each is a blind alley.

After spending a while in denial and offering all sorts of excuses that few people believe, a syndrome of self-abuse develops. This happens so often I wonder if a person feels in some perverse way that self-abuse is an acceptable penalty, self-imposed, for giving up self-control.

COACH'S CORNER:

It is time to "take to the field!"
There is "Power in Numbers!"
Become a winning coach! A Wonder Woman!
Coach other women MVPs, girls, teens and women of all ages!

CHAPTER NINE
THE PLAYOFFS

Obstacle to overcome: SWEATING IN PUBLIC

M — (My)

There is a lot of blood, sweat, and guts between dreams and success.

–Paul Bryant

V — (Victory)

Gold medals aren't really made of gold. They're made of sweat, determination, and a hard-to-find alloy called guts.

–Dan Gable

P — (Plan)

Enjoy your sweat because hard work doesn't guarantee success, but without it you don't have a chance.

–Alex Rodriguez

This descriptive from http://kidshealth.org/kid/talk/yucky/sweat.html

helps us to first understand "sweat" and why we do it...

It's those "kid" coaches again, Man they are smart!

135

You're biking up a hill, pedaling as hard as you can. You're almost there and—what's this? Your back is all wet, and so is your face. Don't sweat it—it's only sweat!

Your body works best when its temperature is about 98.6 degrees Fahrenheit (37 degrees Celsius). When your body gets hotter than that, your brain doesn't like it—it wants your body to stay cool and comfortable. So the part of your brain that controls temperature, called the hypothalamus (say: hy-poh-thah-luh-mus), sends a message to your body, telling it to sweat.

Then special glands in your skin called—what else?—Sweat glands start making sweat. Sweat is also known as perspiration (say: per-spuh-ray-shun), and it is made almost completely of water, with tiny amounts of other chemicals like ammonia (say: uh-mow-nyuh), urea (say: you-ree-uh), salts, and sugar. (Ammonia and urea are left over when your body breaks down protein.) The sweat leaves your skin through tiny holes called pores. When the sweat hits the air, the air makes it evaporate (this means it turns from a liquid to a vapor). As the sweat evaporates off your skin, you cool down.

Sweat is a great cooling system, but if you're sweating a lot on a hot day or after playing hard you could be losing too much water through your skin. Then you need to put liquid back in your body by drinking plenty of water so you won't get dehydrated (say: dee-hi-dray-ted).

Why Does Sweat Smell?

Sweat isn't just wet—it can be kind of stinky, too. But the next time you get a whiff of yourself after running around outside and want to blame your sweat glands, hold on!

Sweat by itself doesn't smell at all. It's the bacteria that live on your skin that mix with the sweat and give it a stinky smell. And when you reach puberty, special hormones affect the glands in your armpits—these glands make sweat that can really smell.

Luckily, regular washing with soap and water can usually keep stinky sweat under control. Many teens and adults also find that wearing deodorant (say: dee-oh-duh-rent) or antiperspirant (say: an-tee-per-spuh-rent) helps.

So don't worry about a little sweat—it's totally normal and everybody sweats. Sometimes too much sweating can be a sign that there is something wrong in the body, but this is rare in kids. If you notice more sweat, it's usually just a sign that it's time to start using a deodorant or antiperspirant. But if you think you have a sweat problem, talk to your parent or your doctor about it.

Updated and reviewed by: Mary L. Gavin, MD
Date reviewed: September 2003
Originally reviewed by: Steven Dowshen

Go Gut

In the big game, every play counts, and that can get us "working up a sweat, alright!"

When the outcome of the game depends on you the pressure to make the right decisions and plays is high. How do you make sure you're calling the right play? The answer is in your gut.

Whether we are aware of it or not, each one of us has a personal team that governs our lives. This team controls the decisions we make, the actions we take, the thoughts we think. We have the power to cut, sign or keep any or all members of our team at any time.

When we worry, fear or doubt, we give our team members free run of our lives. They jump into the huddle and they make their opinions heard loud and clear until we finally just grab one of their suggestions and go with it. Often with reservations, we choose to ignore our own instincts. That's when you find yourself left bruised and battered in the field, trampled by consequence.

When we take time to listen and follow only the voices of the teammates we allowed on our inner all-star team, we will discover some of our greatest advocates for success in whatever we do—our instinctive, intuitive voices.

Find a quiet place where you can be alone and think about the decision you need to make. Now listen to what your inner voice is telling you. All too often, we ignore that "niggle" at the back of our minds. You know the one—it's that little voice that tells us something is not quite right. We either ignore it, or push away those uneasy feelings. We convince ourselves that we're doing the right thing. But how can something be right if it doesn't feel right? If your initial reaction tells you not to do something, then don't.

A bird does not sing because it has an answer, it sings because it has a song.

—"Wonder Woman" Maya Angelou

How do we learn to listen to that inner voice? Practice, practice, practice!

Start with a simple exercise that will help you tune into that gut instinct. The next time you're grocery shopping, you're probably going to have to decide between two different brands of the same product. Maybe one is more expensive, but it's a reputable brand. The other one is on sale for a much cheaper price, but you haven't heard much about its quality. Quick, what product is your gut telling you to choose? It may seem silly but it helps you tune in to your inner voice. Try to incorporate it into daily decisions you make. Is it the black dress or the blue pantsuit—an apple or a banana with lunch today? The more you exercise it, the clearer your voice is going to be.

COACH'S CORNER:

- **Write down the decisions you made today by listening to your gut. Looking back, were they the right choices? Why or why not?**

   Don't worry if you make the wrong decision. You can always fix your mistake. Better yet, you can learn to fix your mistake and you can learn from your experiences. Learning is a curve that leaves us in the straight and narrow.

Here are a few of my favorite points ... There are five here and she has shared them with others in the wonderful and very informative (another big boy) Les Hewitt ... Focus series...!

Now it is your turn to Write your own "series" from MVP lessons, and winning strategies....

A Note From - Our MVP author Coach:

LuAn Mitchell-Halter's Top 5 Success Strategies

Here are a few plays from my own winning playbook. Let's get to work on building yours!

1.Don't Scattershot

Assertive individuals often feel stronger and more relaxed about their goal(s) while aggressive persons create feelings of frustration and stress that affect work performance negatively. The key is to:

Focus—Take Aim—Target Shoot!

2. *Build Alliances, Especially Strong Ones With Yourself, When Questioned*
Even unconventional alliances can "pus" your score up if they make sense! Like the gridiron, there are continual obstacles in life—things that get in your way and attempt to prevent you from reaching the goal line. The biggest challenge facing many in business is social norms that question a person's ability and responsibility. This can be a huge barrier to success, either as an entrepreneur and/or business owner or to any corporate career.

3. *Be True to Your Team! Fly Your Flag! Wear your "True" Colors Proudly*
Corporate Business—much like a sporting event—is a tough game full of cheap shots and winning plays. In the words of a woman who was surely an "all star", Amelia Earhart:
The most difficult thing is the decision to act, the rest is merely tenacity.
The fears are paper tigers.
You can do anything you decide to do.
You can act to change and control your life: And the procedure, the process, is its own reward.
You're already wearing the winning team's jersey. What are you waiting for, let's hit the field.

4. *Keep it REAL! "Real Exciting! Real Life! Real Rewarding!"*
The key to breaking down obstacles and winning the game is mental toughness, and staying alert. To attain a goal, one must always keep your eye on the ball—"the company and objectives,"—and believe in the mission, oneself and the team.

5. When You've Gained Yardage—Recognize The Plays That Worked
Just as important as the challenges we all seize is how we tackle those challenges. Winners here need to develop a framework for their thinking, a framework that calls them to greatness!

CHAPTER TEN
WHO MOVED THE GOAL POSTS?

Obstacle to overcome:
BEATING OURSELVES UP

M — (My)

We just have one basic focus. We are focused on going one direction, and that is forward.

–Michael Johnson

V — (Victory)

Whatever we expect with confidence becomes our own self-fulfilling prophecy.

–Brian Tracy

P — (Plan)

If we did the things we are capable of, we would astound ourselves.

–Thomas Alva Edison

She shoots, she misses?

Women MVP's Learn from Failure:

Noun 1. *goalpost* - one of a pair of posts (usually joined by a crossbar) that are set up as a goal at each end of a playing field

crossbar - long thin horizontal crosspiece between two vertical posts

goal - game equipment consisting of the place toward which players of a game try to advance a ball or puck in order to score points

post - an upright consisting of a piece of timber or metal fixed firmly in an upright position; "he set a row of posts in the ground and strung barbwire between them"

upright, vertical - a vertical structural member as a post or stake; "the ball sailed between the uprights"

Innovation and success can only come from someone with the creativity and courage to try, fail, learn from their failure and keep trying again and again. This is not a life's mission that most women gravitate to naturally. It is difficult for any defeated person to get up and try again but it's even harder for women who are expected to fail and is beat down by the "I told you so" syndrome.

It is on our failures that we base a new and different and better success.

–Havelock Ellis

However, women can be better then men at learning from their mistakes. It's not because women are smarter but because they have the fear of failing again that drives them forward. This fear is invincible.

143

COACH'S CORNER:

- Look at your goal and say it out loud. List reasons why you believe you will succeed in achieving this goal. Continue adding to the list as you work toward your goal.
- Close your eyes and take a few moments to imagine your success. You have achieved your goal. How does it make you feel? How is your life different because of this success?
- List successes you have had so far en route to achieving your goal. How have they made you feel? Keep growing this list, and refer back to it often.

The biggest reason why you shouldn't fear failure is because failure is your best teacher. The key is to learn from your mistake instead of focusing on the fact that you made a mistake. Analyze your actions, identify what went wrong and find a way to correct it. If you don't learn from your failures, you will continue to fail over and over and...well, you get the picture.

- Look back at a memorable failure in your life. (You don't need to worry; we all have at least one!) Describe the failure.
- What went wrong? Did you make a poor decision, or take the wrong action?
- How could you have done things differently?
  NOW DESTROY IT... Burn it (safely or shed it, whatever) Time to let it go, give it up and get on with the show!

You don't have to learn from just your own mistakes—learn from the mistakes of others! This can help ensure you won't make the same mistake, and can also serve as motivation. If so-and-so failed a few times but still found success, then so can you!

Did you know that Michael Jordan, arguably the best basketball player ever to grace the court, was cut from his high school's varsity team?

"It was embarrassing not making that team," he said in an article special to ESPN.com. "They posted the roster and it was there a long time, without my name on it. I remember being really mad, too, because there was a guy who made the team that really wasn't as good as me."

Instead of giving up, Jordan decided he needed to make himself the best in order to continue playing basketball. Arriving at the school at seven o'clock every morning, his high school phys ed teacher would hear the sound of Jordan already practicing in the gym.

"Whenever I was working out and got tired and figured I ought to stop, I'd close my eyes and see that list in the locker room without my name on it," Jordan told ESPN.com, "and that usually got me going again."

Jordan went on to play 1,072 games, log 41,011 minutes on the court and score 32,292 points in his career. He is a five-time regular-season National Basketball Association (NBA) MVP, a six-time NBA Finals MVP, has won six NBA championships and has set many NBA records, including a 30.12 average.

Clearly, someone who has learned from his failures!

COACH'S CORNER: ONE—
Who can you learn from? Let's do some research and find out!

- **Choose some successful people in the field related to your goal. For example, if you're trying to lose**

145

weight, Oprah might be on your list. Write down their names.

- Do some digging on each of these people.

Start by visiting this website if you haven't yet, why NOT www.jimtunnel.com Check out the Internet, the library (back issues of magazines and newspapers) or scan the TV guide for any feature programs about these people. Make notes of any of their failures.

COACH'S CORNER: TWO—

Self-defeating patterns from www.jimtunnel.com - When thinking about how to correct self-defeating patterns, it helps to ask yourself: "What would I think of the choices I have been making if a teenager I loved were making the same ones?"

We don't allow our children to adopt habits that are damaging to themselves or others. All too often, though, we are more lenient with ourselves than we would be with our children. Perhaps this is because we have the mistaken idea that self-defeat is a victimless crime.

One lesson we learn from football is that the more self-discipline you apply to yourself, the better you will be and the better off those around you (crewmates, teammates, etc.) will be. That interaction works in life as well.

The better the example parents give to children, the easier being a parent will be. The better the example a supervisor gives his or her staff, the better the internal communication and outward success of that team will be. The better each spouse tries to meet the "give 100%" rule, the more likely it is that both spouses will reflect the inspiration.

It is a tough truth to comprehend when you are in the mood to be self-indulgent. When self-indulgence wins over self-management, our perspective becomes increasingly narrow and inward. We lose sight of the "big picture."

To prolong hiding from a situation that looms larger than our sense of self, we often miss seeing how small episodes of self-indulgence add up to self-abuse. We don't see how erosion of our will and joy in life can be detrimental to the supportive people around us. Or, if we do, we tend to discount the reason for the fading or increasingly fractious relationships. It's easier to blame our friends instead of our own behavior, even though our behavior is nothing more than the result of our choices.

The ability to continually invent excuses is a clever mind trick.

- Now research these failures. The Internet is probably your best choice as you can "Google" any key words. Did you know that Edison failed over 10,000 times before finally inventing the electric light bulb?
- Read over these failures. What would you have done differently?
- What did you learn from each of their mistakes?

Now, you don't have to make a mistake to learn more about your goal. A good tip is to keep track of your work as you progress, and review it each night. You may spot something that you know isn't going to work and prevent a mistake before it even happens.

There will be those days when you are ambushed by something out of the blue, and you want to give up. Those days are clearly the days that you must get up and move on. And there will be days when something someone says, or a rejection, will bring you to your

147

knees. It is on those days that you focus on taking the high road and maintain what's important.

The bottom line is, at least once in life you are going to get rocked. One of the toughest things to do is to get back up after life has kicked you down. All of these exercises simply prepare you for the inevitable, and remind you of why you want to get up.

As Michael Bennett, a running back with the Minnesota Vikings, recounts on SI.com, "My rookie year I got hit by Bears linebacker Brian Urlacher on a screen play. He came through and cleaned my clock. From my neck down I didn't have any feeling for a few seconds. I forgot where I was. It was terrible. I had to lie there for a little while, wait for my feeling to come back. When I did get up, my head was spinning. He was like, 'Welcome to the NFL, rookie Sarina Russo has built a business from her own failures. I have had the great honor and privilege to have our books published by the same publishing house, her book "Meet me at the TOP… and my first book "Lessons learned from the Impossible dreamer," an honorable and distinguished lady we both admire and are in a distinguished group with took the books into Romania to help to encourage others through the open sharing…When Sarina was only five-years-old, she moved from Sicily to Australia and faced ridicule from her peers and scorn from her teachers who doubted her abilities because her English was poor.

She eventually won everyone over and went on to university but left feeling unfulfilled. She began working as a typist but was repeatedly fired for having an "attitude." Sarina didn't let her failures dim her future. Instead, she switched gears and rented a room above a bank. She started a small typing school and helped her students find work upon their graduation. Her business grew into the Russo Institute of Technology with a campus of over 1,000 students in Brisbane.

CHAPTER ELEVEN
WINNING THE GAME

Obstacle to overcome: LIMITED IMAGINATION

M — (My)

You are not obligated to win. You are obligated to keep trying to do the best you can every day.

—Marian Wright Edelman

V — (Victory)

The superior man makes the difficulty to be overcome his first interest, success comes only later.

—Confusious

P — (Plan)

You need to overcome the tug of people against you as you reach for high goals.

—General George S. Patton

The ultimate key for women to win the game is dreaming big.

Limited
adj.

Confined or restricted within certain limits: *has only limited experience.*

Not attaining the highest goals or achievement: *a limited success.*

Having only mediocre talent or range of ability: *a popular but limited actor*

Imagination

Imagination is, in general, the power or process of producing mental images and ideas. The term is technically used in psychology for the process of reviving in the mind percepts of objects formerly given in sense perception. Since this use of the term conflicts with that of ordinary language, some psychologists have preferred to describe this process as "imaging" or "imagery" or to speak of it as "reproductive" as opposed to "productive" or "constructive" imagination....

en.wikipedia.org

Remember when you were a kid and you dreamt that one day you would be a world-renowned brain surgeon, jetting across the globe to save lives, with the world at your doorstep? And oh yeah, you could eat candy whenever you wanted. Everything was a possibility and the idea that you couldn't have whatever you wanted never even popped into your head.

What happened to those days? What happened to the little girl that imagined all the wonderful things that would one day be hers? Coleman Young said, "We need to dream big dreams, propose grandiose means, if we are to recapture the excitement, the vibrancy and the pride we once had."

I've always said that you can learn so much from children. Well, why don't we try now?

While men tend to be realists, women have the ability, the creativity and the confidence to be dreamers.

Women dream big, which is why they can be big successes. They don't let the obstacles become their downfall because they have the ability to focus on achieving that big dream.

COACH'S CORNER:

Back to the basics from www.jimtunnel.com

When the issues of bad behavior arise in questions from fans or the media, usually concerning the demeanor expected from officials, I toss it back to the basics: Officials are athletes, too. We are in the game because of the ancient code of brave competition and true excellence. It would be a disservice to those standards of discipline and durability for anyone claiming to be an athlete to make an excuse for "losing it."

Now, it's true. Players (and occasionally officials) have been known to display bad behavior. You catch a story about drunk driving; a paternity suit or bar fights. The varieties of bad behavior are as numerous as the options for a copout.

Some say an occasional black sheep in the flock adds excitement and is to be expected, as if that kind of excitement makes a better contest. I don't buy that. It makes no sense to argue than an episode of no-control prepares one for sure control the next time.

On the level of the "pageant playing field" I spoke to the Miss Teen pageant contestants in London, Ontario, and was honored to share inspirational words with this group of dreamers. I'd do just anything to win, anything at all, one hopeful beauty gushed… If I knew no one would ever find out, that is.

Following my speech, a Miss Teen contestant approached me and I told her that up until then, she didn't believe she could be a winner without the crown.

I immediately went to work to help her see differently. I work hard to make it clear to anyone who will listen that the pageant playing field is more than a place to prance around in a swimsuit—it's a chance to share winning stories and share how we can all make a positive difference in the world. These girls are more than beauty contestants—they are up and coming MVPs.

MVPs like Christina Hudson, a 23-year-old advertising student in Michigan. As a 12-year-old, she appeared to be the perfect teenager—an honor roll student, cheerleader and track star. Inside, she was dying. The more she excelled, the harder her single mother had to work to pay to support her success. The guilt caused depression and she began cutting herself. It was years before she eventually stopped. During her healing, she took part in the Miss Teen pageant and won Miss Greater Grand Rapids. Now, she plans to enter the Miss Michigan contest and hopes to one day become Miss America to spread her message. But she knows that even if she doesn't win the crown, she's still a winner because she has healed, inside and out.

COACH'S CORNER:

- Close your eyes and think back to your childhood. I know it may seem more like way back for some of us, but try hard to remember those days. What dreams did you have as a child? Write them down, even if they seem insignificant—if you can still remember how badly you wanted a unicorn when you were six, it must have been important to you.
- Why did you think you were going to achieve those dreams? How did the thought of achievement make

152

you feel?

- Do you have dreams like these as an adult? Why/why not?

Now that we're grown adults, it's time to start thinking like kids. We need to start thinking with limitless boundaries and endless possibilities. Don't worry if your dream seems outrageous—that's half the fun!

- Write down a list of your top ten goals in life. Think BIG! If one of your dreams is to have your own island, then write it down.
- Split your dreams into two groups: "easy" and "impossible."
- Why did you put specific dreams in the "easy" category?
- Why did you put certain dreams in the "impossible" category?

Now, I've kind of tricked you with this exercise. Those of you who have zero dreams under the "impossible" category get it. The whole point of dreaming big is realizing that no dream is impossible to achieve!

- Revisit your list of dreams in the "impossible" category. What ways can you make them possible (or put them in the realm of possible)?

Only those who dare to dream—and dare to dream big—can dare to succeed.

I was honored to be featured in a great book called Surviving Adversity www.survivingadversity.com with this great "Big Boy" MVP! His strength, dignity and stamina are a great Coaching lesson for us all as we "Play to Win," in this "Game of Life!"

On November 17, 1991, Detroit Lions' offensive guard Mike Utley (#60) was paralyzed during an NFL game. His courageous

"THUMBS UP" gesture has become the national symbol of Mike's fighting spirit. In the many months that have followed since his injury, Mike has focused all of his energies towards rehabilitation. This has meant countless hours of therapy which have made Mike nearly 100% self sufficient. Today, Mike has voluntary movement of muscles in his lower legs and feet and participates in a "gaiting" program with the help of leg braces and crutches.

In addition to his own fight to walk again, Mike has now taken on a new challenge...helping all people with spinal cord injuries.

I am proud to be featured with Mr. Utley in a great book featured at www.survivingadversity.com

O.K. Ms. MVP time for you to get "discovered," let's audition for the MVP starring role, where you're the leading lady!

This script from www.imdb.com reminds us of:

HOLLYWOOD VERSES REALITY.... Just take a look at this scene...

"Playing fields of make believe heroes and villains" let's get into "character."

(Reality really is stranger than Fiction)

Memorable "Winning the Game" Quotes from *Dr. No* (1962)
Bond admires a huge aquarium. Dr. No enters

Dr. No: One million dollars, Mr. Bond. You were wondering what it cost.

James Bond: As a matter of fact, I was.

Dr. No: East, West, just points of the compass, each as stupid as the other.

Dr. No: The Americans are fools. I offered my services, they refused. So did the East. Now they can both pay for their mistake.

James Bond: World domination. The same old dream. Our asylums are full of people who think they're Naploeon or God.

James Bond: Both hands on the wheel, Mr. Jones, I'm a very nervous passenger.

Felix Leiter: You Limeys can be pretty touchy about trespassing.

James Bond's first scene, winning a game of chemin-de-fer

James Bond: I admire your courage, Miss...?

Sylvia Trench: Trench. Sylvia Trench. I admire your luck, Mr...?

James Bond: Bond. James Bond.

Professor Dent tries to kill Bond, but his gun is out of bullets

James Bond: That's a Smith & Wesson, and you've had your six.

Shoots Dent twice

James Bond: Tell me Miss Trench, do you play any other games?

James Bond: Don't worry. I'm not supposed to be here either.

Honey Ryder: Are you looking for shells too?

James Bond: No, I'm just looking.

Miss Moneypenny: James! Where have you been? I've been searching all over London for you.

Picks up phone

Miss Moneypenny: 007 is here sir.

Slaps Bond's hand away from the papers on her desk

James Bond: Moneypenny! What gives?

Miss Moneypenny: Me, given an ounce of encouragement. You've never taken me to dinner looking like this. You've never taken me to dinner, period.

James Bond: I would, you know. Only I would be court-martialed for tampering with government property.

Miss Moneypenny: Flattery will get you nowhere... but don't stop trying.

Miss Taro: What should I say to an invitation from a strange gentleman?

James Bond: You should say yes.

Miss Taro: [*shaking her head*] I should say maybe.

155

Worker: What happened?

James Bond: I think they were on their way to a funeral!

Sylvia Trench: When did you say you had to leave?

James Bond: Immediately... almost immediately

Dr. No: That's a Dom Perignon '55; it would be a pity to break it

James Bond: I prefer the '53 myself...

Dr. No: I'm a member of SPECTRE

James Bond: SPECTRE?

Dr. No: SPECTRE—Special Executive for Counter Intelligence, Terrorism, Revenge, Extortion—The four great cornerstones of power headed by the greatest brains in the world.

James Bond: Correction. Criminal brains!

Dr. No: The successful criminal brain is always superior. It has to be!

M: If you carry a oo-number it means you have license to kill, not get killed!

COACH'S CORNER: (check your own ratings)

Put a tape recorder to work for you... record yourself at some point today in a conversation with someone, be natural, and then play it back and type out the transcript... You'll be astonished!

Make a video if you prefer...Your very own reality TV show.

As Underdog would warn, DON'T TOUCH THAT DIAL!

CHAPTER TWELVE
YOU DID IT!

Obstacle to overcome:
NEGATIVE VOICES FROM THE PAST

M — (My)

Success is to be measured not so much by the position that one has reached in life...as by the obstacles which he has overcome while trying to succeed.

–Booker T. Washington

V — (Victory)

Always bear in mind that your own resolution to succeed is more important than any other one thing.

–Abraham Lincoln

P — (Plan)

I advise you to say your dream is possible and then overcome all inconveniences, ignore all the hassles and take a running leap through the hoop, even if it is in flames.

–Les Brown

Winning the game—implementing the game plan and achieving the goal—is exhilarating. There were times when discouragement set in but it was that one mentor who offered advice, encouragement and an example of what a successful businesswoman looks like. Now it's time to return the favor to other dreamers.

Negative:

characterized by or displaying negation or denial or opposition or resistance; having no positive features; "a negative outlook on life"; "a colorless negative personality"; "a negative evaluation"; "a negative reaction to an advertising campaign"

expressing or consisting of a negation or refusal or denial

having the quality of something harmful or unpleasant; "ran a negative campaign"; "delinquents retarded by their negative outlook on life"

reckoned in a direction opposite to that regarded as positive; "negative interest rates"

less than zero; "a negative number"

damaging: designed or tending to discredit, especially without positive or helpful suggestions; "negative criticism"

a reply of denial; "he answered in the negative

veto: vote against; refuse to endorse; refuse to assent; "The President vetoed the bill" minus: involving disadvantage or harm; "minus (or negative) factors"

wordnet.princeton.edu/perl/webwn

Voice:

n.

The sound produced by the vocal organs of a vertebrate, especially a human.

The ability to produce such sounds.

A specified quality, condition, or pitch of vocal sound: *a hoarse voice; the child's piping voice.*

Linguistics. Expiration of air through vibrating vocal cords, used in the production of vowels and voiced consonants.

A sound resembling or reminiscent of vocal utterance: *the murmuring voice of the forest.*

Music.

Musical sound produced by vibration of the human vocal cords and resonated within the throat and head cavities.

The quality or condition of a person's singing: *a baritone in excellent voice.*

A singer: *a choir of excellent voices.*

One of the individual vocal or instrumental parts or strands in a composition: *a fugue for four voices; string voices carrying the melody.* Also called *voice part.*

Expression; utterance: *gave voice to their feelings at the meeting.*

A medium or agency of expression: *a newsletter that serves as a neighborhood voice.*

The right or opportunity to express a choice or opinion: *a territory that has a voice, but not a vote, in Congress.*

Grammar. A property of verbs or a set of verb inflections indicating the relation between the subject and the action expressed by the verb: *"Birds build nests" uses the active voice; "nests built by birds" uses the passive voice.* Also called *diathesis.*

The distinctive style or manner of expression of an author or of a character in a book.

tr.v., voiced, voic·ing, voic·es.

To give voice to; utter: *voice a grievance.* See synonyms at *vent.*

Linguistics. To pronounce with vibration of the vocal cords.

Music.

To provide (a composition) with voice parts.

To regulate the tone of (the pipes of an organ, for example).

To provide the voice for (a cartoon character or show, for example): *The animated series was voiced by famous actors.*

idioms:

at the top of (one's) voice

As loudly as one's voice will allow.

with one voice

In complete agreement; unanimously.

Middle English, from Old French vois, from Latin v?x, v?c-.

I'm actually very ordinary, except people get to pay their money to come watch me work. The same way that we go to McDonald's... we don't care about the guy behind the counter, but if he was doing something special, we'd pay our money to go watch him cook that hamburger.

–"Big Boy" Samuel Jackson

Men are more likely to seek mentors to help them advance their game plans, goals and careers. Whether women don't think of finding a mentor or can't find a suitable mentor (there are still more men in managerial positions than women), they are less likely to find a role model to help them in their business pursuits

Samuel L. Jackson was born on the 21st of December, 1948 as "Samuel Leroy Jackson". Sam Jackson started to become popular after his role in the Spike Lee film, Jungle Fever in 1991 where he played a crack addict. In 1996 he played the role of Jules in Quentin Tarantino's classic film "Pulp Fiction" where he was a dirty mouthed hit man with a philosophical edge. Not only did he earn himself a Oscar nomination for best supporting actor, but he also rocketed himself into Superstar status. His career took off and was able to command large acting fees for films, including $USD10 million for the movie "Shaft" in 2000.

Samuel L. Jackson was born in Washington, D.C and grew up in Tennessee. Jackson suffered from a stutter while growing up and was advised by a speech therapist to audition in a play, which subsequently cured him of his stutter and set his career path for him. He overcame the "negative voices," from his past!

Samuel Jackson is a classically trained thespian actor. He struggled to make it for many years, only playing small roles in films. In the early nineties his career began to take off, playing criminal type roles, usually with plenty of swearing and killing involved. After the Pulp Fiction role in 1996 he was able to choose more commanding roles, often appearing in leading roles as the "action hero" in film like "The Long Kiss Goodnight" and "Shaft".

Jackson has been nicknamed "the King of Cool" and his role as Jules in Pulp Fiction was voted the 2nd coolest movie character of all time by the Empire Magazine in the United Kingdom.

The films he has appeared in have grossed more box office money than any other actor in the history of movies. As of January 2005, Samuel L. Jackson has acted in films that have brought in more than $3US Billion worldwide.

Sam Jackson married his partner and fellow actor La Tanya Richardson in 1980. They have a daughter, Zoe, born in 1982

COACH'S CORNER:

Act 1 Scene one

You are right where you want to be doing what you are called to do and doing it better than anyone!

Now in this "act," we are encouraged by others and their achievements learning from others in all walks of life and is providing an opportunity to lend other girls and women expert advice and personal experience to coach them to success!

Memorable Quotes from *Fat Albert* (2004)

Taken from www.imdb.com

Fat Albert: Hey, hey, hey!

Dumb Donald: Are you ready? 'Cause when I buck-buck, you better duck-duck.

Lead Teen: Are you gonna buck-buck, or are you just gonna talk?

Dumb Donald: Buck number 6, coming!

Runs and jumps on the pile

Lead Teen: Yes! We held! Now we're the buck-buck champions!

Bill: Hold on. We've still got one more guy.

Lead Teen: Bring him out then.

Bill: Come on out, F-a-a-a-at Albert! He loves to hear us call his name.

Fat Albert: Hey, hey, hey! Who wants to play?

Lead Teen: Oh, no! Run! I got a bad back.

Fat Albert: Hey, hey, hey, I said I'm gonna stay.

Bill: Hey, hey, *hey*, friends don't let friends fade away.

Fat Albert: Don't use my lines on me.

Bill: Guys, cut it out.

Salesman: [*after adding up the prices of clothes that Fat Albert tried on*] that'll be $10,428 and 22 cents.

Fat Albert: Uh, I... I don't have any money.

Salesman: Why didn't you tell me that?

Fat Albert: You didn't ask.

The devil has put a penalty on all things we enjoy in life. Either we suffer in health or we suffer in soul or we get fat."

—"Big Boy" Albert Einstein

Woman MVP or NO Woman MVP, Body image is HUGE, it requires a HUGE person to get over past images, or overcome the "ghosts" from negative voices from the past...

Fat paunches have lean pates.

Love's Labor's Lost, I. I

One Woman MVP overcame her negative body image and destructive habits…she brought her present and past into a positive place for her own future and the future of many…

Another MVP—Florine Mark has been helping women just like herself in their pursuit of a healthier body image. Florine, who suffered from a childhood weight problem, joined the only Weight Watchers program in 1963 in New York and lost 50 pounds. Having tried a number of unsuccessful diets, including a near overdose on diet pills, she knew there were other women going through the same struggle she had.

No diet will remove all the fat from your body because the brain is entirely fat. Without a brain, you might look good, but all you could do is run for public office."

–"Big Boy" George Bernard Shaw

In 1966, she opened her first Weight Watchers franchise in Michigan and was once the largest franchise owner. She became President and Chair of the board of the Weight Watchers Group Inc. She is also a motivational speaker who shares her message of hope and inspiration with other women.

This from the "Wonder Woman," at www.florineonline.com

She recently penned her first book, titled: Talk to the Mirror: Feel great About Yourself Each and Every Day which teaches women to love themselves in order to succeed in life.

Things weren't always so great for Florine, she overcame many negatives from her past.

A painfully self-conscious girl who grew up fifty pounds over-weight, poor, and made fun of at school, Florine hated what she saw when she looked in the mirror. It wasn't until her late twenties—fol-lowing a failed marriage, years of painful struggles with debilitating self-esteem issues, and a reliance on diet pills that almost ended her life—that she turned her life around and went on to become one of the most admired businesspeople and motivational speakers in America. In this amazing and inspiring guide to self-empowerment, Florine Mark tells you how she turned her life around, sharing her most intimate experiences and wisdom.

Florine's message is simple: before you change things like your weight, career, social life and relationships, you must learn to give yourself the same unconditional love and support you would give your best friend. With *Talk to the Mirror* as your guide, you'll learn to make friends with that person in the mirror.

COACH'S CORNER:

Whether self-doubt is holding you back, or you feel something is missing from your life, this is the place to feel safe as you challenge yourself with Florine's self-quizzes, exercises, and inspirational stories could help you to discover how to:

- Replace negative self-image with a reflection of the person you want to be
- Treat yourself with unconditional respect, kindness, and support
- Conquer your fears of failure and discover your true potential
- Cope with life's challenges and disappointments
- Achieve your goals—professionally, socially, and romantically

Talk to the Mirror—Feel Great About Yourself Each and Every Day, I encourage you to Look up other "Wonder Women" and learn the "Moves."

When people keep telling you that you can't do a thing, you kind of like to try it!

—"Wonder Woman" Margaret Chase Smith

"Spill it, sister!"

A beautiful woman, black hair swept off a China doll face, looks back at the man nuzzling her cheek. "Pain was too good for him" reads cut-out letters on the coaster's image.

A smiling woman with a checkered apron tied around her tiny waist gestures at food in an open refrigerator. "Get your own damn dinner" the letters spell.

"Wonder Woman" Ann Taintor has taken the 1940s and given it a twist on the playing field.

Combining vintage images of "too happy" men and women with "saucy tags," Taintor interprets what these people are "really" thinking on everything from napkins to magnets.

I have a stash of Taintor's napkins behind the bar in my home, and I have fun dishing them out to guests. One in particular caught my eye. A woman, brown pin curls framing her face and a slim cigarette burning between slender fingers, stared at me from the napkin. "Spill it sister" said the message.

An appropriate phrase, I think, to welcome you to a Life as a Woman MVP.

This is not your typical "how-to" book. Yes, I will show you how to find success in your own life but you have to "spill it" on the workbook pages, adapting my advice and tips to your personal goals. The more work you put into the book, the more the book will work for you. There is no magic wand that will make your dreams come true—only you can do that. Practice makes perfect.

I know what you're thinking. What does she know about my dreams, and how far away they seem? What does she know about what I have to put up with, and the creepy stuff I take on the playing field of life every single day?

Believe it or not, I've dealt with my share of schtuff, on and off the field, and still do for that matter... (News Flash) YOU ARE NOT ALONE; it never really just all "goes away" one day...At least not in my limited experience.

Many before you have been where you've been,, maybe not exactly but similar, and have "put up" and gotten beyond the same things that you have, or are struggling to, and help is available.

I (Like many others) may be a little further down the line of scrimmage now but it wasn't always the case—and money certainly does not make all of life's "schtuff" disappear now, either.

So what do you do when life tries to trip you up? Kicks you in the shins, do you curse and complain, or find ways to get around the obstacles in your way? Does it sound impossible? It depends on how much you want to succeed and what it all means to you.

There are plenty of teams out there, just waiting for the right quarterback to take them to the Super Bowl!

Why not take the lead and become a Woman MVP!

Try these woman MVP winner thoughts on for size, then "suit up" for the big game:

- I am learning more about everything, including how to learn more.
- Love today.
- I make my own coincidences, luck and destiny.
- My future depends on my decisions now.
- The past is the past

166

- What is believed to be true is true for those who "buy into it, and take it to the field." I want to "buy into" the good stuff I know is going to "Win the day, every time!"

I choose now to "buy in" to the belief in my full potential, my very own Good Stuff!

I will not just "pass up" on the opportunity to become all I can be! These winner thoughts are the most common way in which we train ourselves for success under different circumstances. Not everyone uses all of these at once, but we all react differently under different circumstances. Practicing these thoughts is how we condition our behaviors to win.

Life is the most competitive game on the planet. It has high stakes, big consequences and plenty of people watching—and we're expected to navigate through all of its obstacles to find success.

Trust me; it doesn't have to be that hard! All you need is a good coach and a set of plays that will help you score and win this game called life. I've been lucky enough to find personal and business success and I'm going to coach you to do the same.

The five S's of sports training are: stamina, speed, strength, skill, a spirit; but the greatest of these is spirit.

–"Big Boy" Ken Doherty

COACH'S CORNER:

No matter what your goal is, you probably didn't get there on your own. One of the best lessons I learned was to pay attention to those I admire, and to surround myself with excellent people for support. Never be afraid to ask questions! I still look to the people who have the traits, qualities and behaviors that I wish to emulate.

167

Now that you've achieved your goal, why not inspire fellow dreamers? I believe that part of human nature is that we all like to help people, even if it's hidden deep down at the time. If you see someone who can truly benefit from knowledge, be generous and give them your time. A mentor has the opportunity to educate, influence and feel the immense satisfaction of helping someone succeed. All the senses are invigorated and stimulated. To see a person grow and blossom, and know you were a part of that, is a wonderful feeling.

You might be surprised at how much you learn by "coaching" someone. Maybe by refereeing some times and making good calls yourself, you'll prevent someone from being taken advantage of, or from falling when they could have skated past an obstacle.

You're probably thinking, "But what do I know? I couldn't possibly help someone!" Sure you can!

You know more than you think. Besides, a coach is not there to tell another person what to do. A TEAM (Together Everyone Accomplishes More) working together provides guidance, offers advice, answers questions and lends a listening ear together as one unit.

Mentor: Someone whose hindsight can become your foresight.
–Anonymous

COACH'S CORNER:
- **Think about your own mentors those people you admire and want to emulate. Why do you admire them?**
- **What sort of help or inspiration do they lend to you?**
- **Do you think your end result would have been different if you hadn't had these mentors? Why / why not?**

**Having seen all of the wonderful things your mentors
have given you, doesn't it just feel right to pass along
some wonderful things of your own?**

- **Make a list of the top ten things you've learned in
achieving your goal.**
- **List the top five skills that helped you achieve your
goal.**
- **List the top five skills you had to acquire to help you
achieve your goal.**
- **If you could give one crucial piece of advice to someone aiming for the same goal, what would it be?**

Take a look at your answers—WOW!

You've certainly come a long way in your journey. See, I told you
that you know more than you think. Sometimes it's hard to see all
that we've accomplished until we take a step back and really examine our plays and out playing field.

Be open to these opportunities to plant a seed of good, nurture
it, watch it grow and never underestimate your role. Grow, throw a
few... but always give back, more.

Just because you've accomplished one goal, doesn't mean that
the Game has been called.

Bad weather can call a game for some, but you will need to revisit and reconsider before you let it call more.

Flip back to your list of dreams (which should all be listed under
the "easy" category!) and pick one. I have never heard a football
player who has won a Super Bowl say that one is enough. Keep the
hunger and let's start collecting those MVP titles! Make your "tro-
phy cabinet" shine with pride!

Go back to start, collect poem for FREE, rewrite the "Beauty
Tips" for yourself... You are an Official Woman MVP!

The world ain't just your stage anymore, Honey It's your "Playing Field!"

Let the games begin!

The Woman MVP Creed

I _____ have a dream that is truly coming from the core of who I am. And it is connected to my own personal gifts that I came to share with the world. It will burn inside me until it is realized. I am a Most Valuable Person, an unstoppable woman.

Dedication

This Book is dedicated to a TREMENDOUS Champion of all champions "Big Boy" whose belief in Coaching and Motivating Players on the "PLAYING FIELD OF LIFE," has sparked an entire series of All Time GREATS on Winning missions around the world!

My Dear friend and Tremendous Coach extraordinaire... Charles Tremendous Jones... You shall ROCK the Stadium of Life in my heart and soul forever!